D1766955

Religious Education for All

Erica Brown

Illustrated by
Cherille Mayhew

David Fulton Publishers
London

David Fulton Publishers Ltd
2 Barbon Close, London WC1N 3JX

First published in Great Britain by
David Fulton Publishers 1996
Reprinted 1997

Note: The right of Erica Brown to be identified as the author of her work has been asserted by her in accordance with the Copyright, Designs and Patents Act 1988.

Copyright © Erica Brown

British Library Cataloguing in Publication Data

A catalogue record for this book is available from the British Library

ISBN 1-85346-392-2

All rights reserved. No part of this publication may be reproduced, stored in a retrieval system or transmitted, in any form, or by any means, electronic, mechanical, photocopying, recording or otherwise, without the prior permission of the publishers.

Typeset by The Harrington Consultancy Ltd
Printed in Great Britain by Bell and Bain Ltd, Glasgow

Contents

Acknowledgements

Anyone who embarks on a book of this kind is indebted to the people who have been partners in the process and woven into the time-span of the work involved.

Firstly, special thanks to my husband Alan, for his supportive love and shared interest in Religious Education. Throughout the hot summer of 1995 I suspect he often felt his wife was wedded to the script as well as to him! Without his unending good humour, *RE for All* would not have been possible. Secondly, I would like to express gratitude to Barry Carpenter, Director for the Centre for the Study of Special Education at Westminster College, Oxford and to Jo Egerton our secretary for their friendship and encouragement. Also to David Fulton and his team for the privilege of working with them.

Among the many friends who are members of faith communities or scholars in religion, I am particularly indebted to Mr Riadh El Droubie, Mr Dilip Kadodwala, Dr Peggy Morgan and Dr Kanwaljit Singh who read the introductory notes to the principal world religions and offered their help and advice. I should also like to acknowledge the valuable contribution which the SCAA Model Syllabuses for Religious Education have played in providing a springboard for ideas and help in writing parts of the Glossary of Terms.

From the outset of the book, my vision was to encapsulate an exciting and lively approach to teaching Religious Education. Special thanks are due to Cherille Mayhew whose attention to detail in the illustrations has already won the hearts of those who have seen her work.

Lastly, and by no means least, I am indebted to schools and to individual young authors for their inspiring contributions to the book.

Dedication

A book for Katie, her parents and special children everywhere.

Foreword

For too long the insights and innovations of teachers undertaking postgraduate studies or research for higher degrees have been locked in the libraries of Higher Education Institutions. Dormant and inaccessible to the wider teaching profession, they have gathered dust on the library shelves. The potential for dissemination has often been lost, and with it the opportunity for significant ideas relating to classroom practice and effective teaching and learning to reach a wider audience. The wealth of knowledge gained by classroom practitioners through further study warrants a platform for sharing.

In the field of special educational needs where teachers are daily working with pupils with complex and intricate patterns of learning, further educational enquiry, through an advanced course of study, has often illuminated a problem and, what is more, devised a solution that would be of value to a much wider educational audience. Of late, some texts have endeavoured to collate recent and relevant studies for publication, and hence wider dissemination. In particular, the work of Graham Vulliamy and Rosemary Webb (1992) and Gordon Bell (1994), both published by David Fulton Publishers, are good examples of this.

To further endorse this worthy and brave development, a new venture was established in April 1995 between the Centre for the Study of Special Education, Westminster College, Oxford, and David Fulton Publishers. The Fulton Fellowship in Special Education is to be awarded annually. Broadly, it aims to support the research of a teacher not only through the phases of investigation, reflection and critical study, but beyond. Each Fulton Fellow will receive a book contract from the publisher to enable them to take their research beyond purely academic exercise into an accessible text available to a larger professional group, many of whom may be equally curious about the research topic, and keen to hear of the enquiry process undertaken and outcomes identified.

In 1995 the first Fulton Fellowship was awarded to Erica Brown, a teacher and lecturer, known nationally for her work in the area of Religious Education for pupils with special educational needs. Her recent further research into this topic indicated that schools and teachers were struggling with the implementation of Religious Education in the basic curriculum. OFSTED reports have highlighted that the spiritual dimension of the curriculum is receiving scant attention.

Hence it seemed timely that Religious Education should be added to the already successful 'for All' series. Teachers have always grappled with the implementation problems posed by RE in the curriculum, but these difficulties have become particularly acute when considering Religious Education for pupils with special educational needs. A lack of differentiation within the subject has often left pupils as peripheral participants, their spiritual development ignored and their right to receive a balanced curriculum severely in question.

The Agreed Syllabuses produced by LEAs, following guidance from the Schools Curriculum and Assessment Authority (1994) has gone some way towards offering informative guidance to teachers. However, as with all statutory programmes of study, they do not contain sufficient breadth of learning experience for all pupils, and enrichment through extended programmes of study (Carpenter, 1995) is a necessary process for teachers to undertake if we are to engage those pupils with special educational needs in effective and meaningful learning.

Religious Education for All affirms the right of all children to this aspect of the curriculum. If we are to achieve breadth and balance for the whole child then it is sorely needed. Erica Brown's sensitive analysis of children's interactions in the classroom situation draws out the religious dimension of their daily lives and the growth of their spirituality. Her penetrating insights will aid teachers in identifying experiences of this kind: ones that they may not normally identify, and thus will clarify the nature and purpose of Religious Education in the curriculum.

This book is premised on celebration of human life, in all of its forms and manifestations of religious faiths and practices. Religious Education is seen as a curriculum vehicle for promoting self-esteem, encouraging all pupils to value one another, and to see beyond our outward characteristics towards our inner qualities. Fundamentally, RE can nurture those dimensions of a child that will ensure that they are in touch with all aspects of themselves. Indeed, some Agreed Syllabuses have identified the unique opportunity RE offers for celebrating all aspects of a child's talents, and tackling discrimination.

For practitioners working with pupils with learning difficulties and disabilities we are so often alongside those children who are uniquely human, and their 'special needs' are manifestations of that uniqueness. Erica Brown engagingly charts for us how Religious Education can be 'for All'. I suspect in so doing she will cause many readers to reflect upon their own spiritual development. She powerfully reminds us that awe and wonder are to be valued in children's learning: indeed, are they not the source of joy that teaching can offer us all?

Barry Carpenter
Oxford, October 1995

Introduction

'If I had but two loaves of bread, I would sell one and buy hyacinths, for they would feed my soul,' wrote the thirteenth-century poet, Sa'di.

Seven hundred years later, as I walk down a school corridor, the figure of a child through an open door captures my attention. She is about seven years old and she is moving towards the corner of the room where a piece of blue Chinese silk forms the backcloth for a display. A ray of sunshine highlights the folds of the fabric and she reaches out her hand. Squatting down she bends forward to examine a piece of gnarled bark and, tracing the grooves with her fingers, she croons softly. Her left hand extends to a bowl of wedgwood blue hyacinths and then, grasping the pot firmly in both hands, she lifts it until she is able to bury her entire face in the scented blooms. I reflect on Sa'di's words and know without a doubt that Melanie agrees with him.

Religious Education in England and Wales has occupied a unique balance between national and local interests for many years. Under the 1944 Education Act it was the only subject in the curriculum which was required by law and the only subject for which special local arrangements were made. For pupils and their teachers in all sectors of education the last two decades have contained mixed blessings. At a time when the content and quality of the curriculum have been under critical review and subjected to dramatic changes the religious and spiritual needs of young people have been highlighted. Indeed the opening clauses of the Education Reform Act require the Curriculum for all maintained schools to :

'promote the spiritual, moral, cultural, mental and physical development of pupils at the school and of society and... prepare such pupils for the opportunities, responsibilities and experiences of adult life. [Clause 1.2.b]

The Education Reform Act 1988

The Education Reform Act (1988) (ERA) reaffirmed many of the statutory requirements of the 1944 Education Act whilst at the same time amending or introducing new requirements for LEAs and schools. The discussions on Religious Education and school worship take up more pages in Hansard than any other single topic.

The Education Act sets out as the central aim for the school curriculum that it should promote the:

spiritual, moral, cultural, mental and physical development of pupils and of society, and prepare pupils for the opportunities, responsibilities and experiences of adult life.

The Aims of Religious Education

Religious Education aims to give young people opportunities to develop their knowledge and understanding of religion and to contribute to the development of their own beliefs and values. The stated aim for Religious Education in DFE Circular 1/94, which was published to clarify the 1988, 1992 and 1993 legislation on Religious Education and collective worship, is:

RE in schools should seek to develop pupils' knowledge, understanding and awareness of Christianity, as the predominant religion in Great Britain, and the other principal religions represented in the country; to encourage respect for those holding different beliefs; and to help promote pupils' spiritual, moral, cultural and mental development. (paragraph 16)

This understanding of Religious Education involves the whole personality. There is knowledge to be learned and there are skills to be developed; there are attitudes to be encouraged and emotions to be explored; there is self-understanding to be nurtured and developed and an identity to be fashioned; there are personal beliefs to be formed.

In the early years of children's development Religious Education is primarily concerned with three areas:

* spiritual development
* knowledge and understanding of religious belief and practice
* opportunities to explore and to reflect on religious and life experiences.

Statutory Requirements

The Education (Schools) Act 1992 requires HMI Chief Inspector of Schools to keep the Secretary of State for Education informed about Religious Education and the spiritual, moral, social and cultural development of pupils via the four-yearly inspection of schools.

The requirements are as follows:

- Religious Education must be provided for all registered pupils.
- The term 'religious instruction' used in the 1944 Education Act is replaced by 'Religious Education'.
- Parents retain the right to withdraw their child from Religious Education.
- Religious Education must be taught according to a locally agreed syllabus prepared by an Agreed Syllabus Conference made up of representatives from the LEA, teachers, the Church of England (not in Wales), and other Christian denominations and members of other world religions present in the area. Representatives of grant maintained schools in the area may also be included.
- Religious Education must not be denominational although teaching about denominational differences is permitted.
- Any new locally agreed syllabus must reflect the fact that the religious traditions in Great Britain are in the main Christian whilst taking account of the teaching and practices of the other principal religions represented in the country.

Special Schools

Pupils in special schools are referred to in the Education Act 1993, which states:

Every pupil attending a special school will, so far as is practicable, attend collective worship and receive religious education unless the child's parents have expressed a wish to the contrary. It is for the schools to decide what is practicable but, in general terms, the Secretary of State would expect the question of practicability to relate to the special educational needs of the pupils and not to problems of staffing or premises.

Religious Education in the School Curriculum

Religious Education is a statutory part of the Basic Curriculum although, unlike the National Curriculum, it is administered at a local rather than a national level. It also has equal standing in relation to the core and other foundation subjects although, again, it is not subject to nationally prescribed attainment targets and assessment procedures.

The Principal World Religions

Although legislation does not define which principal religions should be taught, it has come to be accepted that all principal religions in Great Britain should be included and children should learn about and from the religions studied. Traditionally, there are six major world religions, namely: Christianity; Islam; Hinduism; Buddhism; Sikhism; Judaism. However it should also be recognised there are other faiths represented in Great Britain, for example Confucianism and Taoism and the Rastafarians have large numbers of adherents, together with smaller numbers of Baha'is and Jains.

Model Syllabuses for Religious Education

In 1993, the Secretary of State for Education wrote to Mr David Pascall, chairman of the National Curriculum Council, asking the NCC, and subsequently the School Curriculum and Assessment Authority (SCAA), to produce Model Syllabuses for Religious Education. In 1994 SCAA published two Model Syllabuses for Religious Education which were the result of lengthy and painstaking work between representatives of the six major faith groups in England and Wales to outline the central core of their religion. Although these documents are not statutory and they are intended to provide guidance to Agreed Syllabus Conferences and SACREs (and not schools), many new syllabuses reflect the content of the models, including Programmes of Study based on the beliefs and practices of Christianity and the other principal religions.

RE for All affirms the important contribution Religious Education makes to the education of *all* pupils, regardless of ability, family background, race or creed. Through a differentiated teaching approach which has been carefully planned using the *Model Syllabuses* as a general framework, it seeks to contribute to a curriculum in schools which is balanced, broadly-based and relevant to children growing up in a rapidly changing world. The text is supported by suggested activities or learning experiences and examples of children's work from a range of special schools. The content is particularly appropriate to Religious Education Co-ordinators and non-specialist teachers of Religious Education to pupils at Key Stages 1 and 2. Statements of Achievement as a foundation for Key Stage 1 are included as a framework for very young children or students who may need extra support in their learning.

Through 'setting the scene', providing a focal point for attention and opportunities for sensory experiences, the classroom activities are essentially practical ones. Colleagues are urged to use the content as they prepare for inspection of Religious Education and as a springboard for their own ideas and teaching approaches. The philosophy of the book is that, taught well, Religious Education is relevant to the present and future experience of *all* children. But perhaps most importantly of all *RE for All* expresses the whole-hearted view that Religious Education offers young people hope and promise in a world which often neglects the spiritual dimension of life and in turn underestimates human potential.

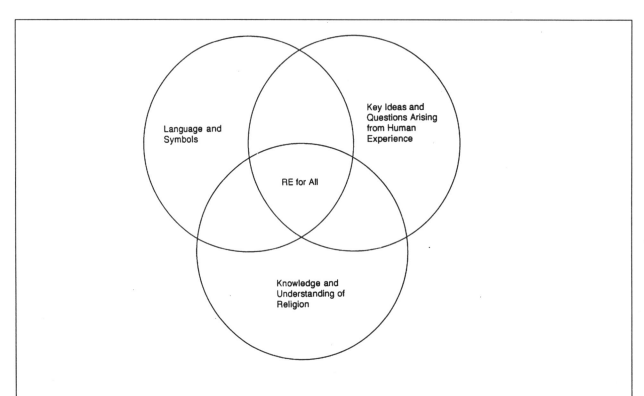

Understanding religion demands that children learn 'about' and 'from' the beliefs, values and customs which underpin the faiths studied. The scheme of work and framework of assessment uses the two Attainment Targets: 'Knowledge and Understanding of Religion' and 'Key Ideas and Questions Arising from Human Experience'. The two Attainment Targets may be achieved through the Learning Experiences provided which are underpinned by nine study units. Language and symbols play an important part in helping pupils to understand how religious belief and practice are expressed.

CHAPTER 1

Religious Education For All Children

Starting with the Children

'One Monday morning I was in a classroom as the children arrived. Dawn approached me where I was helping a child unbutton his coat and she thrust a note in my face. In it her Mum had written about a family event at the weekend. The message wasn't very clear but I understood there had been a party with lots of food (and drink!), Dawn's baby sister had lots of presents, and I should look in Dawn's bag for a candle. I deduced it had been a Christening and a search in the bag confirmed this. Meanwhile, the classroom door burst open and Stephen entered like a whirlwind, made straight for the home corner, picked up a doll by her leg, flung her above his head and announced, "Being the new Daddy!" While the register was marked Nadia climbed onto my lap and, taking my hand, she twisted round my wedding ring and signed to me that her Mum had one just like it. On the way to assembly, Dilip conveyed in no uncertain terms that he didn't like sitting on the hall floor, he had no intention of behaving and I suspected that if he was challenged he would create more disruption than he had already planned!'

Every teacher will meet situations like these. Whether we are prepared for them or not, children bring with them experiences which are broadly religious. And it is our professional responsibility to build on these life experiences so that they nurture children's religious and spiritual development. For Dawn, her experience of a Christian rite of passage is the beginning of understanding something of religious practice, shared family occasions and a special meal.

For Stephen it is the third 'new' Daddy of the year and he needs to role play the event in order that he may begin to make sense of the dilemmas which he is facing. Nadia's family belong to the Hindu faith and she is able to convey her recognition of symbolism as she twists my ring. She will need help understanding how promises are made and rings are exchanged by people from a variety of faith traditions. And we have all encountered children like Dilip. Assembly should not be confused with school worship or Religious Education, but, if through Religious Education we strive to help children to develop self-esteem and positive attitudes towards other people, we owe it to Dilip to help him to realise that life is all about choices and decisions, many of which are made by other people on our behalf. The lessons which are learned extend far beyond the formal curriculum and our starting point should be where the children are, rather than where we should like them to be.

Is Religious Education for All a Problem or a Possibility?

In spite of the lengthy deliberations which took place when the Education Reform Bill (1987/1988) was going through Parliament, and the many responses to the legislation of ERA by Agreed Syllabus Conferences, SACREs, SCAA and members of world faith communities, the matter of Religious Education which is accessible to all pupils has not been documented in detail. Some Agreed Syllabuses produced after ERA offer a very few lines of guidance such as:

> Pupils in special schools should, as far as is practicable, receive religious education unless the pupil's parent wishes the child to be withdrawn. [The Agreed Syllabus for Religious Education in East Sussex, March 1993]

> Special schools will be expected to implement the Programmes of Study and assessment arrangements of this Agreed Syllabus so far as is practicable. [The Agreed Syllabus for Religious Education in Avon, 1993]

Other Agreed Syllabuses are more helpful:

> Religious Education offers a unique opportunity and responsibility to recognise and develop each person's talents and to tackle discrimination in whatever form it appears.

> Religious Education provides opportunities for imaginative, flexible and sensitive teaching of pupils of all abilities. In mainstream school teachers need to be aware of the particular needs of the pupils with special educational needs and should

develop strategies and resources to provide support for such pupils. Teachers and schools need to address the issue of differentiation and accessibility of materials and their presentation. [The Agreed Syllabus for Religious Education in the London Borough of Hounslow, 1992].

Most Agreed Syllabuses for Religious Education are united in the view that, in the early years of pupils' religious and spiritual development, teaching should be relevant to children's life experiences whilst also encouraging an awareness and understanding of the belief and practice of religion.

Among the few educationalists who have written about Religious Education for *all* children is Flo Longhorn. Referring to pupils whom she calls 'very special', she says special schools provide a relevant environment in which children can stretch, reach and attain their full individual potential. Religious Education, she believes, can help this process by revealing 'a deeper dimension to life'. Furthermore she goes on to suggest 'Areas of Prominence' (see table).

Dowell and Nutt (1995), building on the work of Brown (1991; 1993), have emphasised the importance of helping children in special schools towards a greater awareness of themselves and other people. They believe this can be encouraged through activities 'in class, in the whole school and in the wider community'. Goss (1995) shares this view and he charges teachers of pupils with profound and multiple learning difficulties 'to attempt to recognise emotional and spiritual needs within the curricular and social experiences provided'.

Are the Aims of Religious Education the Same for All Pupils?

Although the format of Agreed Syllabuses varies, most state the aims of Religious Education as quoted in the Education Reform Act. Some also provide more clearly defined objectives, which are related to Key Stages and reflected in Statements of Attainment.

However teachers interpret aims, it is essential that the Religious Education curriculum includes teaching which helps children to learn *about* religion as well as learning *from* religion. It is also essential that clear links can be made between what is taught in Religious Education and the remainder of the curriculum. The Dearing review of the National Curriculum (1995) contains both explicit and implicit mention of religious and moral themes, such as respect and concern for the natural world in science, and pattern and order in mathematics.

Perhaps the greatest lesson is that the aims of Religious Education must be sufficiently broad to be relevant to all pupils regardless of their ability and their religious or cultural background. Furthermore, the whole curriculum supported by the ethos of the school should assist pupils in their spiritual and moral development.

Should Schools Provide for Differentiation in Religious Education?

A differentiated approach to learning which treats pupils as individuals should apply in Religious Education. It should also allow the teacher to provide appropriate teaching strategies for groups of pupils.

The Code of Practice (1994) requires Individual Education Plans (IEPs) to be used in the planning, implementation and review of pupils' learning in order that they are able to achieve at the highest levels of which they are able. In Religious Education this will include:

- the delivery of carefully structured teaching approaches
- providing imaginative learning experiences which arouse and sustain children's interest
- supporting the learning which takes place in Religious Education by what is taught in other curriculum areas.

What is the Role of the Class Teacher?

Making Religious Education accessible to all pupils will be dependent on appropriate teaching and learning strategies. Success in learning depends greatly on the learning environment and the quality of the relationship between the teacher and the pupils, including an understanding of their different levels of emotional, social, physical and intellectual maturity. Motivation for children will come from the very positive effect of having someone who wants to listen to (or to watch) what they have to say or how they choose to communicate.

Of all the factors which affect the way in which children learn, the most important, yet difficult to describe is the atmosphere which exists in a school, and especially in the classroom, where pupils are expected to commit themselves in a personal way and where their responses and ideas are exposed to the view of other people. There is no room for falsehood. Our youngsters know exactly what our values are and whether we accept them for who they are or not. They sense our emotions and are aware of the 'language' we speak with our bodies as well as with our voices. They are sensitive to such things as gesture; posture; tone; manner and ritual. It is a sobering fact that a young person's view of what happens in the classroom is sometimes quite different from that of the teacher.

However we choose to evaluate the way in which we interact with pupils and encourage them in their learning, we should set ourselves high standards and make time to reflect on questions such as:

Areas of Prominence in Religious Education for the Very Special Child

• Awareness of "me"	feelings, emotions, senses, awareness of reactions to events
• Awareness of others	relationships at school and home and within the community, awareness of the needs of others and achievements, stages of life, from cradle to grave
• The needs of myself	beginning to recognise own worth, self esteem, achievements, privacy, acknowledging a range of positive and negative feelings, choice, accepting oneself, being able to communicate "no" and to know that it is respected, a purpose in life
• The needs of others	awareness of worth and self esteem in others, caring, sharing, giving, acknowledging the rights of others to have different feelings
• The world around me	awareness of the beauty and uniqueness of the natural and man-made world, the sensory world, caring for the natural and man-made world
• The numinous sense	developing the sense of mystery and wonder, extending sensory awareness into unknown territory, awareness of religious feelings, curiosity
• Celebrating life	awareness of personal events, school events and home events, awareness of festivals and celebrations, both secular and religious exploring the common elements of religion
• Reflecting on life as a whole	stillness, privacy, awareness of being alone, awareness of belonging, meditation, awareness of other life styles

Reproduced from *Religious Education for Very Special Children*, Flo Longhorn (1993)

- Do I always show concern for each pupil, encouraging a sensitivity towards other people and the forming of relationships?
- Does my teaching provide the potential for pupils' spiritual development in the classroom, the school and in their daily lives?
- Does my teaching allow pupils to make their own responses and to explore their own experience?
- Does my teaching provide a variety of situations where I strive to communicate at the child's level?
- Do I always show an appreciation of the contribution which each young person has to make, letting them know effort is as important as success?
- Do the expectations which I have of individual children's learning, motivate them to achieve?

What is the Role of the Religious Education Co-ordinator?

In order to ensure that the content of the curriculum is well planned, it is usual for a member of staff to be given responsibility as the Religious Education Co-ordinator. This role is many faceted and will involve professional judgements about the most appropriate and relevant delivery of the subject as well as supporting teachers in their own classroom practice. Some of the principal responsibilities of the post holder will include:

- Enabling the school to agree a policy statement for Religious Education, and to develop a curriculum which indicates how the Programmes of Study and Assessment are to be delivered.
- Regularly reviewing the policy statement and the curriculum.
- Ensuring Religious Education features in the School Development Plan.
- Keeping well informed of current thinking and developments in Religious Education including attending in-service training and disseminating information to the head teacher, members of staff, governors and parents.
- Keeping well informed about current resources available for Religious Education and building up teaching and learning resources in the school.
- Liaising with colleagues from other schools from which pupils may come or go.

CHAPTER 2

The Spiritual and Moral Dimension of the School Curriculum

The National Curriculum Council Discussion Paper on Spiritual and Moral Development (1993) argues that spiritual development is 'fundamental to other areas of learning'. The word 'spiritual' is defined as:

> ...something fundamental in the human condition, which is not necessarily experienced through the physical senses or experienced through everyday language. It is to do with the search for meaning and purpose in life and for values by which to live.

In the context of religion this may include beliefs, a sense of awe, or transcendence. But spirituality is also part of all of us – it is to do with the very essence of *what it means to be human* and in this sense it includes self-understanding and self-worth, creativity, emotional responses, a personal quest for meaning and purpose and forming relationships. In schools it is essential we strive to develop the spiritual dimension, without compromise to the beliefs or integrity of individual persons or faith communities.

How Can a Child's Spiritual Development be Nurtured?

Teachers will need to find opportunities for pupils to explore:

- personal value, uniqueness and worth
- feelings and emotions
- relationships
- the local and wider environment
- commitment (e.g. how it might feel to belong to...)
- awe and wonderment
- periods of quiet, reflection, relaxation
- responsibilities.

The opportunity for Religious Education to contribute to pupil's spiritual development will extend far beyond those things which are taught in the formal curriculum. It will include providing a variety of experiences which give potential for the development of: an awareness of self; an awareness of other people; an awareness of the natural world and the world around; an awareness of religious belief and practice such as learning how people celebrate key events in their lives.

Awe and Wonder in the Classroom

All Agreed Syllabuses produced since the Education Reform Act (1988) charge teachers to give pupils opportunities to experience awe and wonderment. But they seldom suggest how this might take place within the busyness of school life. Certainly we cannot guarantee children will either encounter awe and wonderment for themselves or that the learning situations which we provide for them will lead them to respond in the way which we intended. What we can do however is to provide a kaleidoscope of experiences which may encourage young people to make an inner response.

Richard has cerebral palsy affecting his whole body. He has little voluntary control of his limbs and in many ways he is like a captive bird. The cage is his body, yet he has a tremendous desire to communicate, to learn, to please and to achieve. He cannot use spoken language but when his teacher is with him in the classroom she has no doubt that his love for the natural world shows a spiritual awareness and a response to life. In the springtime he likes to be taken outside to watch the daffodils as they sway in the breeze and to feel the smoothness of the mossy bank where they grow as he is placed to lie amongst the flowers. Sitting in his chair under the old oak tree on a hot sunny day he croons with delight as the dappled shadows move across his twisted body. And autumn never gives way to winter before he has delighted in being rolled in the crisp leaves. When winter comes he bangs his elbows loudly on the tray of his chair until he is taken to the window where he can watch the birds as they flock to their feeding place. (Reproduced from 'Circles of Growth' by Erica Brown in *PMLD Link*).

Finding situations where children like Richard encounter feelings of awe and wonderment do not happen by chance. They demand a willingness on behalf of adults to stand alongside pupils so that we are able to share in their emotional responses. This will be made possible by inviting pupils to experience awe and wonderment through situations which have potential for:

- helping them to enter into experiences and then to focus on the experience at a greater depth
- helping them to discover new facets of those things which they take for granted
- encouraging their amazement about their own bodies and the natural world
- keeping alive in them and in ourselves the intensity of childhood.

Moral Development

The National Curriculum Council Discussion Paper (1993) lists moral values which schools should uphold. These include 'keeping promises' and 'telling the truth'. However there is little guidance given in the document about moral education, although the OFSTED Framework for the Inspection of Schools (1993) describes moral development as being concerned with:

...pupil's ability to make judgements about how to behave and act, and the reasons for such behaviour.

There can be little doubt that the moral development of pupils is influenced by the environment in which they learn. The ethos of every school should support children's religious, spiritual and moral development, regardless of home background, race or creed. It is a philosophy which celebrates the best in life but also acknowledges those things which are harder to come to terms with, and recognises that to be human is a challenge – but it is also a gift.

Both spiritual and moral development involve:

- consideration and evaluation of inner feelings
- reflecting on personal values, attitudes and beliefs
- a sense of healthy self-esteem and personal worth
- personal codes of behaviour.

In the context of Religious Education these elements may be explored from a personal stance and through learning about belief and practices in world religions.

Chailey Heritage Special School in East Sussex reflect their school ethos and moral values in a Charter of Children's Rights (reproduced below with their kind permission) which states: 'wherever a child is, whoever they are with, whatever they are doing, they have the following fundamental rights':

Being valued as an individual
 – being valued for and treated as unique
 – being talked to and about by my own name
 – being consistently cared for across settings
 – being encouraged to be me
 – being given enough time to take part, to do things for myself, to understand and to be understood

Being treated with dignity and respect

– being addressed with respect; never being referred to, or about, as if I am a disability; nor as if I am one of my needs; nor as if I am a piece of equipment; nor finally, as if I am hardly a child at all
– being involved in conversations; never being talked about as if I am not there
– having my privacy reflected at all times and in all places
– having all information about me treated carefully; kept safe and shared only with those people who need to know; never discussing me in the presence of another child
– being given the best possible care that can be provided
– being involved in decisions that affect me; being actively encouraged to express my views and where these cannot be taken into account to be told why

Being loved and cared for as a child

– having the same rights and choices, and, as far as possible, the same kind of life as other children of the same age and culture
– consistent care from staff who really care about me and know me well
– being actively supported as part of a family; having my parents fully involved in any planning for me and acknowledged as ultimately responsible for me
– having access to communication equipment at all times, and being listened to and heard when I need to communicate, even if it takes a long time, and I am not easy to understand
– being given information about what is happening before it happens; being given explanations of procedures before they occur
– being given opportunities to play

Being safe

– not being exposed to unnecessary risks
– being protected from abuse: physical abuse includes any physical punishment or rough handling; emotional abuse includes malicious teasing and taunting, unjustifiably ignoring me, controlling me through fear, shaming or humiliating me or deliberately misinterpreting my communication; sexual abuse includes any sexual act or contact with me
– being part of a service that is integrated; not having to hear things which may undermine my faith in the service as a whole
– knowing that I have all these rights, all of the time I am at Chailey Heritage School, and that these rights can only be denied with good cause
– knowing that all the important adults in my life are aware of these basic rights and being clear about what I can do if these rights are infringed or not respected.

I can smell the different colours of flowers.

I have a Soft feeling When it is quiet.

CHAPTER 3

Principles into Practice

According to DES Circular 3/89: 'Religious Education has equal standing in relation to the core and other foundation subjects'.

In order to ensure that the content of the curriculum is well planned, it will be necessary to have a policy statement for Religious Education.

All schools need to include a policy statement for Religious Education in their prospectus. This statement should be approved by the Governors.

It is recommended the Prospectus Statement is as clear and concise as possible. It should give information about:

- the importance of Religious Education in the religious, spiritual and moral development of the child
- the legal requirement which the school has to provide Religious Education according to the Education Reform Act 1988. *NB* It is suggested that special schools refer to the Education Act 1993
- the aims of teaching Religious Education as stated in DfE Circular 1/94
- parents' rights to withdraw their child from Religious Education and an invitation for parents to discuss their concerns with the head teacher before a request to withdraw a child is made
- how Religious Education is organised in the school and how the school Religious Education curriculum uses Programmes of Study suitable for pupils of different ages and abilities
- the amount of curriculum time spent teaching Religious Education at each Key Stage and the kind of resources available.

Documentation for Religious Education

In addition to a school prospectus statement, OFSTED require a Religious Education Policy Document. The document should contain:

- the aims of Religious Education. In special schools these do not have to agree with the aims stated in the Agreed Syllabus for Religious Education, although often schools prefer to use the Agreed Syllabus as a broad framework
- the legal requirements (as stated in the Education Reform Act 1988) which the school has to provide Religious Education. *NB* It is suggested special schools also make reference to the Education Act 1993
- how Religious Education is organised in the school and the time allocated in each Key Stage
- how the Religious Education curriculum is planned, managed and taught and the cross-curricular dimensions of RE
- how pupil progress is assessed, recorded and reported
- the standards to be achieved
- how the individual learning needs of pupils are catered for
- the right of teachers to withdraw from teaching Religious Education
- the right of parents to withdraw their child from Religious Education
- an outline of the Programmes of Study at each Key Stage
- the resources available.

Finding Out What is Already Being Done in School

In order that the current provision for Religious Education may be assessed, schools may find it helpful to consider some of the following questions:

– Is there a school policy statement for Religious Education and is this included in the school prospectus? Are parents informed of their right to withdraw their child from Religious Education?
– Do the aims of the school stated in the prospectus support *all* children in their religious, spiritual and moral development?
– Is there a Religious Education Co-ordinator who takes responsibility for Religious Education on behalf of other teachers? What are the Religious Education Co-ordinator's qualifications, and is provision made for their in-service training?
– Is there a curriculum or scheme of work for Religious Education in the school?
– How does the curriculum match the legislative requirements for Religious Education and the Agreed Syllabus?
– Do the schemes of work ensure a broad and balanced curriculum with opportunities for differentiation in learning?
– How is pupil progress assessed and recorded? Are the Statements of Attainment or Level Descriptors integral to the learning process?
– How much curriculum time is given to Religious Education? (The Dearing review recommends a minimum of 36 hours per year at Key Stage 1 and 45 hours per year at Key Stage 2.)
– Is the morale of teachers in the school such that they are happy and confident to teach Religious Education?

Drafting and Introducing the Policy

The audit of current provision for Religious Education in the school should provide the framework for the school policy. A consultation period for the draft policy is necessary so that every one involved feels their views are heard and taken into account. It will be important to keep an educational perspective which supports the legal obligations but which also reflects the views of parents and community members.

Once the document is agreed, it should be circulated as widely as possible to ensure that all concerned recognise it as the *school policy*. To this end, the curriculum and practice must consistently and clearly reflect the document. However, it is important that the discussion process is an ongoing one which allows for new initiatives and developments.

CHAPTER 4

The Scheme of Work for Religious Education

In order that the Religious Education taught in a school reflects a curriculum which is broad and balanced, the content will need to be planned carefully whilst also being relevant to the life experiences and individual learning needs of pupils. This cannot happen unless teachers are prepared to stand alongside their pupils and to meet them at their point of learning. A scheme of work is an essential tool in the planning process but if it is to meet the specific needs of individual children it will have to be interpreted and implemented creatively through the opportunities for learning which are provided. A scheme of work will only provide signposts towards children's learning. The teacher must travel alongside children so that they achieve milestones along the way.

The School Development Plan

Schools will need to create and implement a Religious Education Development Plan. This should reflect the replies to the questions suggested in the audit of current provision. The development plan will also need to take into account financial considerations such as providing resources, and show priorities and time-scales.

The SCAA document *Planning the Curriculum at Key Stages 1 and 2* (1995) suggests three stages for the effective planning of National Curriculum subjects. Because teachers are familiar with this model *RE for All* uses the same format.

Long-term planning

Long-term planning is the responsibility of the head teacher, staff and school governors although the Religious Education Co-ordinator may be asked to draft a scheme of work which shows how the Programmes of Study will be developed at each Key Stage. It is important that the Religious Education Co-ordinator in special schools decides which elements of the Key Stage Programmes of Study are best suited to the individual learning needs of pupils. Although it is unlikely that all the elements of the Programmes of Study suggested in this book will be taught in their entirety, it is essential that the content reflects a broad and balanced approach to learning.

Medium-term planning

Class teachers have responsibility for medium-term planning although it is the responsibility of the Religious Education Co-ordinator to provide support. In special schools the Religious Education Co-ordinator has a particularly important role in helping colleagues to plan schemes of work from the Programmes of Study and in helping them to record children's progress according to Statements of Attainment or Level Descriptors.

Planning a scheme of work will include:

- identifying the concepts, attitudes and skills to be developed as learning outcomes
- identifying learning experiences which will support the development of the desired concepts, attitudes and skills
- taking into account the range of pupil ability within the class
- the past and present experience of pupils
- planning for differentiation in learning
- taking into account the family backgrounds of children
- planning a range of experiences and activities which will encourage children in their learning and provide opportunities for teachers to assess progress

- evaluating pupil progress through the Attainment Statements or Level Descriptors
- evaluating the scheme of work, paying particular attention to how the individual needs of pupils are being met.

Short-term planning

Short-term planning involves class teachers considering which aspects of the scheme of work are to be taught and the learning strategies to be used.

Planning a Broad and Balanced Scheme of Work

The content of the school's scheme of work should be clearly identified and documented. Although special schools do not have to follow an Agreed Syllabus for Religious Education, it is important that what is taught contributes to a broad and balanced curriculum. A broad and balanced Religious Education curriculum will include the range of beliefs and practices of Christianity and other principal world faiths. Therefore RE For All suggests an approach to Religious Education which reflects the SCAA Model Syllabuses for Religious Education on which many new Agreed Syllabuses are likely to be based.

The Programmes of Study contain two important Attainment Targets:

1 A knowledge and understanding of religious belief and practice

For children to begin to understand something about the belief which lies at the heart of religious practice they will need opportunities to learn *about* religion as well as learning *from* religion. In other words, we should strive to help them to understand that religion is about what people do as well as what they profess. This will include enabling pupils to experience how religious belief can be expressed through the creative arts such as art; music; story; dance; movement and posture. It will also include learning about the Bible and other sacred books; artefacts; symbols and religious buildings.

2 Key ideas and questions arising from human experience.

Pupils will need opportunities to be actively involved in Religious Education so that from the earliest times they are encouraged to respond to their learning in a way which nurtures the development of skills which are investigative, evaluative and expressive. They should be encouraged to develop positive attitudes and sensitivities towards other people, for example, through reflecting on what it might mean to be a Christian, Muslim, Hindu etc.

Objectives
Foundation for Key Stage 1

In the very early stages of children's religious and spiritual development it is important to provide a foundation on which to build an increasing awareness of themselves as individuals and of relationships with other people. Helping pupils to respond to different environments and giving them a wide range of opportunities to experience sensory learning will provide a framework for developing attitudes such as delight or curiosity, or skills such as reflection or meditation. Children should learn through using their senses and share experiences which enable them to become aware that people, objects, symbols, places, food, and occasions have special importance.

Key Stage 1

At Key Stage 1, Religious Education should strive to build on children's understanding of themselves and their experiences of family life and relationships. Some children will have had direct experience of religious practice; some will have had occasional experience of religion, others none at all. Therefore it is important that teachers take the variety of children's experience into account when planning schemes of work. All pupils should learn from the attitudes which they encounter in school that they are personally valued whilst also beginning to discover the contribution which other people make. They should become increasingly aware of things which are special and important to themselves and other people.

Children will benefit from opportunities to develop their awareness of the local environment through journeys and visits and by having a chance to experience awe and wonderment in the natural world. They should be introduced to symbolism in religion and hear stories about the lives of key figures and religious leaders.

Pupils should be encouraged to celebrate their own achievements and milestones as well as joining in a variety of occasions when people meet together for worship and festivals. Some pupils will find it very difficult to enter imaginatively into the experience of other people and they may need help in order to be aware of the needs and desires of their peers and their teachers.

Key Stage 2

Key Stage 2 should enhance the opportunities and experiences which pupils have already encountered in order that they may build on their knowledge and understanding of religion and increase their spiritual and moral development. Children should be developing a greater understanding of themselves and an awareness of the needs and feelings of other people from a variety of faiths and cultures. They should be given an opportunity to interact with the natural world and the local environment. By the end of Key Stage 2, pupils should have been helped to explore a range of religious ideas and themes including how these are communicated through sacred writings and symbols. They should have heard stories about the life and teaching of Jesus and other religious figures and have been given opportunities to consider their own questions and concerns arising from the Programmes of Study. Their knowledge of religious belief and practice will grow through activities such as visiting places of worship and meeting people from religious communities.

Which Religions should be Studied?

At Key Stage 1, SCAA recommend the Programme of Study should focus on Christianity and normally one other principal religion. At Key Stage 2, teaching will concentrate on Christianity and usually two other principal religions. Mainstream schools must reflect the guidance given in the Agreed Syllabus. In special schools, children's learning should be planned to meet their needs and it is the responsibility of the school to decide which faiths should be studied in addition to Christianity.

Areas of Learning or Study Units

In order that children are given a broad and balanced curriculum *RE for All* suggests nine study units which are contained within the two Attainment Targets (see above).

- Human Experience
- The World Around } including lifestyles
- Special People/Key Figures and Leaders
- Special Books/Sacred Writings
- Special Buildings/Places of Worship
- Festivals and Celebrations
- Special Times/Rites of Passage
- Special Journeys/Pilgrimage
- Sign, Symbol and Language

The first two areas which are concerned with Human Experience and The World Around, are included in the Programmes of Study under the Attainment Target 'Key ideas and questions arising from human experience'. This lays the foundation for beginning to explore other dimensions of religion through some of the suggested Learning Experiences. In the early years of children's spiritual and religious development these study units may contain little which is explicitly religious at all. Nevertheless they provide an essential framework for understanding religion. It is impossible for a child to begin to understand the needs of other people or to appreciate different lifestyles unless he or she has developed an understanding of self.

The remainder of the study units are included under the Attainment Target 'Knowledge and understanding of religious belief and practice' and, in some cases, Symbols.

Keeping a Record of the Schemes of Work

Outlines of schemes of work are included in *RE for All* (see chapter 6, etc). The content of each suggested scheme is described under four headings which include the two Attainment Targets, together with Learning Experiences and Symbols. Teachers should enter the appropriate Key Stage at the top of the planning sheet and highlight what they plan to teach, taking into account differentiation in children's learning.

CHAPTER 5

Developing Concepts, Attitudes and Skills

Pupils should benefit from Religious Education in a number of ways. Increasing their knowledge and understanding of religion is of course important, but it is also essential that this goes hand in hand with the development of concepts, attitudes and skills. Although many of these will also be developed across the whole school curriculum, there are some which ought to permeate Religious Education in particular.

Concepts

In order that pupils are given opportunities to develop conceptual understanding in Religious Education they will need opportunities to help them to explore ideas and to reflect on their learning. All concepts have the potential to be developed at different levels.

Foundation for Key Stage 1

At the Foundation for Key Stage 1 children need to be helped towards concepts of **value and worth**. In the early stages of religious development this will include an awareness of their own needs and those of other people. Being aware of special times and how these are marked in their own families and at school provides children with a foundation for the concepts of **community** and **celebration**. And hearing stories and beginning to realise the worth of special objects may provide a foundation for understanding the concept of **symbolism.**

Key Stage 1

At Key Stage 1 teaching should provide the potential for helping children to develop ideas of:

- value and worth
- celebration
- community
- worship
- ceremony
- authority
- symbolism.

Children will need to be actively involved in the experiential dimension of religion in order that they may begin to develop these concepts. Joining in festivals and celebrations, encountering practices and customs and hearing music and listening to stories will all help to communicate the feelings which underlie what religious people say and do.

Value and worth

Concepts of value and worth might be developed through helping children to understand that certain people, objects, times and places are of special importance to themselves and to other people.

Celebration

A concept of celebration may begin with giving pupils opportunities to reflect on special occasions in their own families and experiencing shared special times at school and in the local community.

Community

Helping pupils to develop an idea of belonging to their own families, to a class, the school family, or perhaps to a club, will provide a base for reflecting upon the fact that people are often linked by shared views, interests or beliefs.

Worship

Visiting religious buildings and exploring how they are used will help pupils to develop a concept of the importance of worship for some people. Sharing special food will also provide an opportunity to develop a later concept of sacred meals.

Ceremony

Giving pupils opportunities to see how people use gesture, action and dress for special reasons may help develop a concept of ceremony.

Authority

Reflecting on the roles which different people have, and how some people influence others, will provide the foundation for a later understanding of the authority of religious figures and leaders.

Symbols

All children will encounter signs and symbols in their lives. Helping them to be aware that stories, words and objects can have special meaning will be the start of developing a concept of symbolism.

Key Stage 2

At Key Stage 2 teaching should provide the potential for helping children to develop ideas of:

- value and worth
- celebration
- community
- worship
- faith
- the ultimate
- ceremony
- authority
- symbols.

At first, these ideas will arise from pupils' own experience. It is the role of the teacher to help pupils to extend this experience so that new and more complex concepts are developed. Religious belief and practice have a deeply personal dimension and for pupils to develop an awareness and understanding of other people they will need to have opportunities to explore what people do and why they do it. Story-telling, role play, meeting members of faith communities and visiting places of worship will give pupils an opportunity to:

- *interpret* or make sense of what they learn
- *evaluate* or consider what they learn
- *apply* or build upon what they learn to enrich their own experience.

Throughout the Programme of Study for Religious Education at Key Stage 2 children's conceptual understanding should be developed by providing opportunities to:

Value and worth

Reflect upon things on which people place value and meaning, for example religious buildings and artefacts.

Celebration

Recognise that there are special times and occasions in people's lives which are marked in distinctive ways.

Community

Understand that a feeling of 'belonging' is important to many people, and that belonging to a community or a group demands responsibilities.

Worship

Understand that many people express reverence and allegiance to a faith through actions and behaviour.

Faith

Understand that for many people religious beliefs are important.

The Ultimate

Reflect upon the fact that many people believe in God.

Ceremony

Reflect upon how ritual is used by some people when they join in religious ceremonies.

Authority

Be aware that religions often have leaders and special books which influence the way in which people live their lives.

Symbols

Be aware of ways in which religious symbols are used to express belief.

Attitudes

All areas of education are concerned with helping pupils to develop positive attitudes. There are however those which it is particularly important to foster in Religious Education. These will include:

- self-understanding
- respect
- fairness
- sensitivity
- empathy
- openness

They might be described as attitudes towards: self; other people; the world around and religion. The development of attitudes is not a linear process and may be difficult to evaluate as a learning outcome.

Foundation for Key Stage 1

In the early stages children will be aware of attitudes through their own experiences and through the examples which other people show towards them. It is important that teachers identify which particular attitudes they wish to nurture in pupils whilst also being realistic in what they hope to achieve.

Key Stage 1

At Key Stage 1 pupils should be beginning to develop **self-understanding** and a **sensitivity** towards the needs of other people. Through their life experiences they should be encouraged to take notice of and to **respect** the feelings of others. This might be helped through opportunities to listen to stories from different religious and cultural traditions, recognising similarities and differences in the points of view expressed by members of the class group, or meeting people from different faiths and visiting places of worship.

Key Stage 2

Throughout Key Stage 2 children should be encouraged to develop confidence to express their own views. They should be helped to establish personal codes of behaviour and values, including an awareness of right and wrong and **fairness**. They should be helped to feel confident about their own religious and cultural backgrounds whilst also respecting similarities and differences amongst their friends. In this way they will be helped to see diversity and difference as potentially positive rather than threatening.

Skills

There are skills to be developed in all areas of the curriculum but in Religious Education pupils will need to develop particular capacities which are about expression, observation, investigation and communication. These skills need to be applied to pupils' learning and it is important for teachers to help children to develop the capacities through the learning experiences which they provide. Suggestions for learning experiences are outlined on the Programme of Study sheets.

CHAPTER 6

Setting the Scene for Learning Activities

'Setting the scene' for Religious Education will directly influence the way in which children become active participants in their learning. Often, schemes of work place emphasis on helping pupils to develop concepts, skills, knowledge and attitudes. Of course these are important elements in the learning process, but providing an environment in which they can be nurtured is the key to success.

RE for All aims to 'set the scene' for children's learning through providing a focal point for attention and suggesting activities which invite children's interest in a number of ways. Although the limitations and constraints of individual schools will determine how teachers plan and resource Religious Education, most classrooms can be organised so there is an area of floor space large enough for the pupils and their teachers to sit in a circle.

The learning experiences which are developed from the schemes of work outlined in the book use examples of religious artefacts, everyday objects and things from the natural world, displayed on a circular cloth. The illustrations often reflect the content of several lessons.

Most activities are concerned with helping children to develop a knowledge of religious belief and practice. Others focus on human experience themes, such as death and dying, where key ideas and questions from children's own experience are explored. Teachers will need to adapt the displays and the activities to suit the individual needs of the children. There will be times when part of a display might be used to develop cross curricular themes, such as the activity on water which might also be used for science. Other occasions may lend themselves to exploring a single object.

The Activities

All the suggested activities and learning experiences have been used in classrooms. Non specialist teachers may find the introductions to the principal faiths useful, together with the notes which develop the theme of the learning experiences in more detail. The suggestions are not exhaustive. They are merely representative of resources which have been used successfully.

Easter

Easter is the central and most important festival of Christianity. For the early Christians, Easter was the only annual festival celebrated, but the first day of each week soon became a thanksgiving when the resurrection of Jesus was remembered in the service of the Eucharist. Associated with the festival of Easter are themes such as:
• new life
• birth
• hope
• joy
• triumph
• forgiveness
• light/darkness.

Easter
Key Stage

KNOWLEDGE AND UNDERSTANDING OF CHRISTIANITY (including belief and practice)
Christian belief expressed through the accounts of Holy Week, the Passion narratives, the Resurrection.
The cross as a symbol for the Christian family.
Key Christian values: forgiveness; self-sacrifice; love.
The celebration of Easter which demonstrates that Jesus is special for Christians.
Stories of Easter which emphasise the theme of 'new life'.

LEARNING EXPERIENCES
Pupils could:
Share feelings of being let down by friends.
Encounter an Easter celebration and share experiences of celebrations they enjoy.
Listen to and respond to the Easter story told through art, music, dance, poetry.
Look at and explore Christian artefacts, and find out about their symbolism, e.g. Paschal candle, Easter garden, cross/crucifix.
Visit a local Christian place of worship/look at a video of a church. Talk about the commercialisation of Easter.
Talk about signs of new life around them in spring and new beginnings.
Cook and taste Easter foods.
Share feelings related to experiences of awe, wonderment, mystery.

Use a time of quiet to reflect on the Easter story.
Talk about how the Easter story relates to experiences in their own lives, e.g. joy, sadness, betrayal.

KEY IDEAS AND QUESTIONS ARISING FROM HUMAN EXPERIENCE
Pupils should be encouraged to think about:
Making and breaking friendships.
Celebrations and special occasions which occur annually.
Things which make us happy/sad.
People we admire – what are their qualities?
People who have brought new life to others, e.g. Helen Keller, Martin Luther King.
Signs of new life in the world about them and new beginnings.
Foods eaten on special occasions.

SYMBOLS
The cross: the crucifix and the empty cross.
Easter garden.
Easter eggs.
Palm crosses.
The Eucharist: bread and wine.
Light and darkness.

Scheme of Work: Easter

It is important that children explore some of these if they are to have some understanding of Good Friday and Easter Day in the Gospel narratives.

The Gospels present the events of Holy Week and Easter from different points of view. Although the accounts and the details differ, most of them are remembered in churches during the services the week before Easter Day. The notes are brief and teachers will need to look up the references for more detail.

Palm Sunday

(Mark 11: 1-11; John 12: 12-16) Palm Sunday is the Sunday before Easter which marks the arrival of Jesus in Jerusalem. Palm crosses are distributed in some churches and there are often processions where people wave palm branches to recall how the crowds laid palm and olive branches at Jesus's feet.

Wednesday of Holy Week

(Matthew 26: 1-16; Luke 22: 1-6 & 7-30; John 12: 1-8) In churches where oils remain which have been used to anoint people at baptism, confirmation, ordination or death, these may be burnt in readiness for new oils consecrated by the bishop of the diocese on Maundy Thursday.

Maundy Thursday

(Matthew 26: 47-56; Luke 22: 7-30 & 39-43; John 18: 1-11) This day celebrates the institution of the Eucharist at the Last Supper. After a Eucharist service in church any remaining consecrated bread and wine is taken to a special altar of repose. Sometimes a priest will wash the feet of members of the congregation as Jesus washed the feet of his disciples. In preparation for Good Friday, in some churches the altar may be stripped, leaving a bare table, and the congregation will leave the building in silence.

Good Friday

(Matthew 27: 1-61 & 69-75; Mark 15: 1-47; Luke 23: 1-56) On Good Friday in some churches services are held which include a commemoration of Jesus's journey to the cross. Some churches hold a vigil from noon until about three o'clock as a reminder of the time Jesus was on the cross.

Holy Saturday – Easter Eve

(Matthew 27: 62-66) In preparation for Easter Day, churches are cleaned and in many traditions they will be decorated with spring flowers. In some communities a cloth of gold and white or silver and white will be placed on the altar. A late night service may also be held where a fire is lit outside the building and a large paschal candle is carried into church where it will burn until Ascension Day. Christians who attend this service usually renew their baptism vows.

Easter Day

(Luke 24: 1-9; Matthew 28: 1-10; John 20: 1-18) Easter Day celebrates the resurrection of Jesus. Church services are joyful and many will include a celebration of the Eucharist. During the service the priest may proclaim, 'Christ is risen', to which the congregation responds, 'He is risen indeed'.

Signs and symbols of Easter

Eggs

For Christians, eggs symbolise rebirth or the resurrection of Jesus. At one time they were a forbidden food during the fasting period of Lent and fresh eggs were exchanged as gifts when the fast was over. Today many people celebrate Easter by giving chocolate eggs. Sometimes a basket of these is blessed by the priest at the Easter Day service and they are given to the congregation when they leave church. In some parts of Great Britain there are traditional games using eggs, such as egg rolling where contestants roll them from the top of the hill and the winner is the person whose egg rolls the furthest without cracking. In parts of Europe sugar and chocolate eggs are hidden in gardens for children to find.

The cross

The cross is the central symbol of Christianity. Christians believe Jesus died on a cross (as seen on a crucifix) and rose from the dead (the empty cross). In some churches Christians kiss the cross as a sign of devotion, or make the sign of the cross, touching their forehead, chest and both shoulders. In many churches crosses are covered during the period of Lent. There are many different types of crosses.

Hot cross buns

Hot cross buns are eaten on Good Friday. They are rich and spicy. A cross marked on the top reminds Christians that Jesus died on a cross.

Passion flower

The passion flower is a native of South America and where it is grown in Great Britain it will often flower much later than Easter. Traditionally the separate parts of the flower are said to tell the story of Jesus's crucifixion. The centre represents the nails with which Jesus was fixed to the cross. The centre of the flower has five deeper coloured areas which are symbols of the wounds in Jesus's hands, feet and side. The outer part of the flower is a symbol of the crown of thorns put on Jesus's head. The ten petals are sometimes said to represent the ten faithful disciples, not including Judas Iscariot who betrayed Jesus and Peter who denied him. The twisting tendrils of the stem are a symbol of the whips of the people who mocked and taunted Jesus during his passion.

Objectives

- To encourage children to experience the sights, colours, smells and tastes associated with the celebration of Easter
- To help children develop an understanding of how religious beliefs and insights are expressed in symbolism and the importance of the cross for Christians
- To help children develop an understanding of the significance of Easter for Christians
- To help children reflect on their own experience of celebration at home/school and in the wider/religious community
- To help children towards an understanding of the themes which lie at the heart of the Gospel narratives

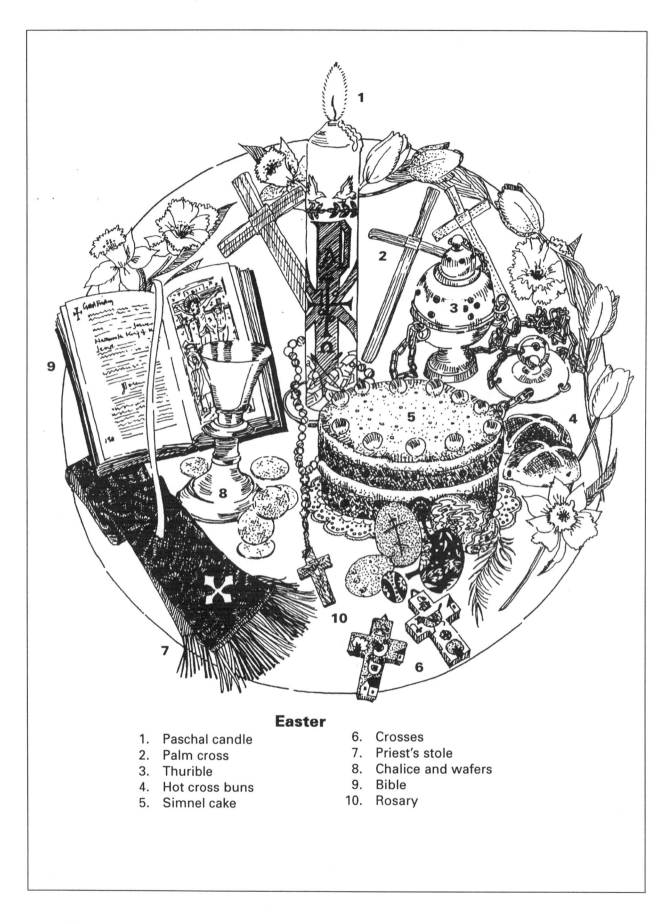

Easter

1. Paschal candle
2. Palm cross
3. Thurible
4. Hot cross buns
5. Simnel cake
6. Crosses
7. Priest's stole
8. Chalice and wafers
9. Bible
10. Rosary

SIMNEL CAKES

225g plain white flour
pinch salt
1 tsp. baking powder
1 tsp.ground cinnamon
150g hard margarine
150g soft brown sugar
3 beaten eggs
2 tsp. lemon juice
1 tsp. orange juice
150g sultanas
100g raisins
50g mixed peel
50g glace cherries
450g marzipan
apricot jam

1. Place paper cake cases in bun tins.
2. Sift the flour, salt, baking powder and cinnamon in a bowl.
3. Cream the margarine and sugar until light and fluffy.
4. Alternately stir a tablespoon of beaten egg and a tablespoon of flour into the mixture.
5. Add any remaining flour and the fruit juice.
6. Stir all the fruit into the mixture.
7. Place one teaspoon of the mixture into each cake case.
8. Roll out small pieces of marzipan into circles and lay them on top of the mixture in the cake cases.
9. Place another teaspoon of mixture on top of each of the marzipan circles.
10. Cook in a pre-heated oven at 170°C, 325°F for about 20 minutes or until the mixture has shrunk away from the sides of the cases.
11. Roll out the remaining marzipan and using a fluted edged pastry cutter the same size as the cakes, cut out circles of marzipan.
12. When the cakes are cool, brush with a little apricot jam and place a marzipan circle on top.
13. Make any left-over marzipan into small balls and place on top of the cakes, securing each with a spot of jam.

HOT CROSS BUNS

250g plain white flour
pinch salt
pinch mixed spice
1 tsp. cinnamon
25g brown sugar
25g margarine
sachet easy mix yeast
1 beaten egg
30ml milk
50g currants
25g mixed peel
For the paste:
1 tbsp. flour
1 tbsp. milk
1 tsp. oil

1. Grease a baking tray.
2. Sift the flour, salt and spice together into a bowl. Add the sugar.
3. Rub in the margarine and add the yeast mixed with milk, as directed on the sachet. Stir, and add the beaten egg and fruit alternately. Mix to a smooth dough.
4. Turn the dough onto a floured surface and knead for 5-10 minutes until smooth and elastic.
5. Place in a greased bowl and cover. Leave for 30 minutes.
6. Mix all the ingredients for the paste together and beat well. Place the paste into an icing bag with a 5mm nozzle.
7. Divide the risen dough into pieces and shape into buns.
8. Place the buns on the trays and pipe a cross on each.
9. Bake the buns in a pre-heated oven at 200°C, 400°F for about 30 minutes.

Resources

- A large white circular tablecloth or similar
- Evergreen and spring flowers
- A paschal candle (a large white candle with a transfer bought from a Christian bookshop is ideal and less expensive); matches
- A selection of Christian artefacts, e.g. chalice and wafers, palm crosses, crucifixes/crosses, small prayer-book, Bible
- Hot cross buns (see recipe)
- Simnel cakes (see recipe)
- Easter eggs
- Hard boiled eggs in their shells

Preparation before the activity

Bake hot cross buns or warm ready-made buns in the oven.
Bake simnel cakes and decorate them.

Setting the scene

Display the white cloth in a central area of floor space. Place the evergreen and flowers around the outer edge and the paschal candle in the centre of the display, surrounded by the Christian artefacts and Easter symbols.

The activity

Ask if anyone knows what the special display on the cloth is about. Encourage responses which show the children's awareness of springtime; symbols and special food. Explain that the candle is a symbol of a special occasion. Can anyone think of any other times when candles are used? Talk about a child who has recently had a birthday with .... candles on a cake. Explain that this is not a birthday, but just as some families have birthday parties and share special food, the Christian family celebrates the festival of Easter by lighting a special candle with the year of the festival on it. Sometimes they share special food too. Draw pupils' attention to the different kinds of crosses which are represented, making special mention of the palm crosses and the pastry cross on the buns. Talk about friends and how it feels if friendships are broken.

Give each child a spring flower and encourage them to smell the perfume and to feel the fragile petals against their skin. Take a hard boiled egg and hold it against the children's cheeks so they are able to feel the coolness and the smoothness of the shell. Allow each child to smell the spicy warmth of the hot cross buns and share the special food among the class 'family'.

Sensory learning experiences

Using the display described in the activities for Easter, which is also illustrated in the drawing, pupils might be encouraged to participate in learning experiences and to explore Christian artefacts.

- Hold a **palm cross** and feel the texture of the palm against your cheek.
- Smell the palm.
- Enjoy the smell of the lighted **paschal candle** and watch the dancing flame.
- Pick daffodils and tulips and feel the smoothness of their delicate petals against your hand. Smell the perfume.
- Taste an unconsecrated wafer and notice how it melts in your mouth.
- Feel the coolness of an egg shell against your cheek.
- Watch incense lit in a **thurible** and enjoy the heavy smell.
- Knead hot cross bun dough and make separate pastry crosses to go on top.
- Smell the spicy aroma of warm hot cross buns.
- Roll marzipan into small balls to decorate the top of the simnel cake.
- Toast the top of the marzipan on the cake and watch it turn golden brown and bubble.
- Wear the priest's stole and enjoy the fabric against your neck.
- Put a rosary around your neck or over your arm and notice the beads are in different groups and shapes.
- Help to decorate the shells of hard boiled eggs.

Infant Baptism

Infant baptism is usually carried out when a child is a few months old. This includes a naming ceremony where the child is given a Christian name and signed with the symbol of the cross. In some churches this is done by a priest; in others by a member of the church. Some Christian traditions choose godparents who make promises on behalf of the child which s/he will affirm at confirmation. A boy has two godfathers and one godmother, and a girl has two godmothers and one godfather.

When babies are baptised in Roman Catholic and Anglican churches, a priest either pours or sprinkles blessed water over the baby's head. In the Greek Orthodox church, babies are dipped into water three times as a symbol of belief in the Trinity (God the Father, Son and Holy Spirit).

Anglican churches usually have a special container for the water used at baptism. Sometimes this is a font, which is often found near the entrance of the church. Other churches have a small bowl which is placed on the altar or table at the front of the church where the baptism ceremony takes place.

Members of the Baptist church are baptised as adults in a pool or tank built into the church floor. This is called the 'baptistery'. With the help of the minister or members of the congregation, the person who is to be baptised

Baptism
Key Stage

KNOWLEDGE AND UNDERSTANDING OF CHRISTIANITY (including belief and practice)

The Church as a Christian community and a building.
Using the Bible: in public services; in personal devotion.
Key Christian values: courage; forgiveness; self-sacrifice; commitment; love; justice.
Important Christian ceremonies: weddings; confirmation.
Special leaders: priests; ministers; elders.
People who have set an example of Christian faith.
Jesus represented as 'The Light of the World'.

KEY IDEAS AND QUESTIONS ARISING FROM HUMAN EXPERIENCE

Who am I? – Being special.
The importance of belonging to a group/family.
Signs of new life in the world about them in spring and new beginnings.
How we welcome people.
Rules and why they are important.
Commitment towards keeping promises.
People who love and care for them and people whose example they would like to follow.

SYMBOLS

Water.
Dove.
Baptismal candle.
Font.
Bible.
Baptistery.

LEARNING EXPERIENCES

Pupils could:

Share ideas about the importance of names and look up their names in a book of first names.
Consider the importance of rituals and ceremonies in life, e.g. birthdays, anniversaries.
Look at and carefully handle Bibles, e.g. a family Bible.
Signs of new life in the world around: new beginnings.
Share feelings about belonging to a group.
Make a display of objects and symbols associated with Christian worship.
Visit a variety of Christian places of worship and learn the names of the key features, e.g. font, table/altar, pulpit.
Listen to and respond to the story of Jesus' baptism.
Encounter Christian celebrations including a baptism and share experiences of celebrations they enjoy.
Listen to stories about Christians past and present.

Scheme of Work: Baptism

---

is dipped completely under the water as a sign that their sins are 'washed away' and they are making a new start. This is called 'total immersion'.

Some Baptist and Free churches hold a service of thanksgiving to God for a new baby, and they dedicate the parents and the child to God, promising to give the child a Christian upbringing.

For all Christians who perform infant baptism, the ceremony is symbolic of cleansing from sin and acceptance into the family of the church. It is also performed in remembrance of Jesus's baptism by John the Baptist in the River Jordan (Matthew 3: 11–16).

John the Baptist taught that people should repent for their sins and start a new life. As a symbol of the beginning of a new life, the followers of John the Baptist were immersed in the River Jordan as a sign that their sins had been 'washed away'. Jesus was baptised and, throughout the centuries, Christians have been baptised in a ceremony which marks a new beginning, following in the way of Jesus. The word 'baptism' means 'immersion', but Christian rituals using water vary and do not always involve immersion.

Objectives

It is hoped that children will:

- reflect on special occasions in their own lives
- begin to develop an understanding of the importance of initiation ceremonies within religions
- develop an awareness of the events within a community which are significant to its members.

Resources

- A large circular tablecloth
- Baptism photographs borrowed from the children's families

Infant Baptism

1. Baptism candle
2. Baptism cake
3. Baptism clothes
4. Baptism gifts
5. Orders of service
6. Water
7. Cross

- A display of baptism artefacts, e.g. a certificate, baptismal candle, Christening robe, baptism cards
- Copy of the story *From Me to You* – see chapter 9 under the heading Myself and Relationships.
- Several pieces of card with the following words or symbols written on them:
  - special clothes
  - special things
  - a special place
  - a special welcome
  - a special name
  - a special baby
  - a priest/minister/vicar
  - parents
  - godparents
  - church family
- A video showing a font or a large picture or slide.

Setting the scene

Place the display of symbols of baptism (including a lighted candle) on the cloth so that they become a focal point for attention. Have the video or slide/picture of the font close to hand.

The activity

Greet the children in a way which is familiar to them, paying particular attention to their names. Comment about how special our names are to us and to other people. Ask whether anyone can guess what the theme of the activity is today? Give a brief introduction to the topic which includes mention that not all Christians are baptised as babies. Share the photographs of baptisms. Show the video or the picture/slide and talk about a font and comment that Christians today continue to welcome people into the church through a service of baptism. Sometimes this happens as an adult, but more often as a baby. If children have visited a church, remind them of the experience and especially how they explored the font. Share the story, *From Me to You*.

Ask pupils if they have any 'special' objects in their homes which have belonged to their families for a long time. Introduce children to the items on the display and explain simply the symbolism of water and light in Christianity. Talk about special clothes; special objects; a special welcome; a special name; special people; special place; special baby; priest/minister/vicar etc, and add the words or symbols to the display.

End the activity by drawing attention to the children's names once more.

Sensory learning experiences

Using the display which is illustrated in the drawing, pupils might be encouraged to participate in learning experiences and to explore Christian artefacts.

- Carefully look at the baptism clothes and notice how tiny they are.
- Explore the shape of the cross with your fingers.
- Watch the curving beauty of the candle flames.
- Look at the greetings cards and notice the pictures on them. Find any symbols which match the pictures on the cards.
- Look at the glass jug of water. Move close to the jug and notice how clean the water looks.
- Pick some pink or blue summer flowers and put them in a vase. Smell the flowers.
- Carefully open the prayer book and find the baptism service. Put the ribbon marker at the first page of the service.
- Share a cake decorated with icing.

Eucharist

The most characteristic act of worship in Christian churches is a sacred meal known by various names: Eucharist; Holy Communion; The Lord's Supper; Mass; Breaking of Bread.

RICHARD REMEMBERS HIS BAPTISM

"My church, Bloomsbury, is a very nice place. I was baptised there four years ago, when I became like a Christian. My family all came to the worship of the church..... I wore special clothes - white shirt and cream trousers and just feet. Maurice Johns led Barbara into the water - it was open. Then he took me to the baptismal water. I go down the steps; Barbara was preaching. My hands together on my tummy Barbara said 'Father, Son and Holy Spirit take me', and I was baptised. Barbara tip me over under the water. My brother came in the water and helped me, wrapped me up to keep me warm. I changed my clothes.

Afterwards all my family in the porch in front of the church - my father took photographs. Then we come back down stairs and everyone helped celebrate of me - with nice cards and presents.

I am a member of the church. I like the communion service. I wear a little cross to show I am a Christian." ❏

(Richard's text is unchanged)

First published in *RESPECT,* journal of The Special RE Network

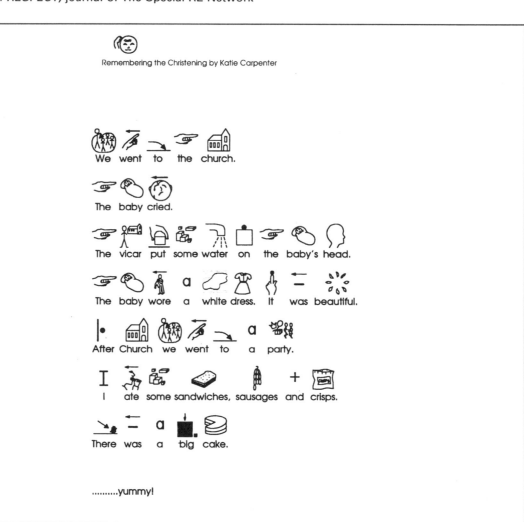

Remembering the Christening by Katie Carpenter

We went to the church.

The baby cried.

The vicar put some water on the baby's head.

The baby wore a white dress. It was beautiful.

After Church we went to a party.

I ate some sandwiches, sausages and crisps.

There was a big cake.

..........yummy!

Eucharist

The word Eucharist means 'thanksgiving'. Christians follow Jesus's example by giving thanks for the bread and wine which are the fruits of the harvest and the work of humankind. They also give thanks for the gift which Jesus gave of himself at the Last Supper and on the cross.

Holy Communion

The sharing of bread and wine emphasises the fellowship of all those who believe in Jesus.

The Lord's Supper

This emphasises the way in which Christians meet together to obey the command of Jesus to: 'Do this in memory of me'. The word 'supper' is representative of 'fellowship'.

The Breaking of Bread

This title describes the worship of Christians today who follow the example of the first Christians who 'spent their time in learning from the apostles, taking part in the fellowship, and sharing in the fellowship meals and prayers'. (Acts 2:42)

Mass

The word Mass is probably taken from the Latin word 'missa' which means 'ended' or 'finished'. The Mass is a sacred meal of thanksgiving which shows the unity of the church through Communion with Jesus.

During the acts of worship the congregation usually receive token amounts of bread and wine as a means of 'communion' with one another. Christians believe that by doing this they are following the instructions of Jesus to his disciples at the Last Supper (Mark 14; 12-26; Luke 22:7-28; Matthew 26: 17-30). The bread is usually in the form of small unleavened wafers, or small pieces of a loaf. Some groups of Christians prefer non alcoholic juice to wine.

Not all Christians use the sacrament – e.g. The Salvation Army and the Society of Friends. The format of the service varies widely between different Christian groups.

The Orthodox Church

In the Orthodox tradition those who are to receive Holy Communion gather in the centre of the church. The wine is administered by the priest from a chalice into the mouth of each communicant. The priest says the name of each person to whom he administers the sacrament. It is usual for Orthodox Christians to fast before receiving Communion.

The Baptist Church

In the Baptist tradition the bread and wine is blessed by the minister and administered by deacons. Members of the congregation pass the plate of bread from one to another, each person taking a piece and consuming it immediately. Non alcoholic wine is administered in individual glasses and consumed as a corporate act to symbolise that Christians are the body of Christ who share in communion together.

The Roman Catholic Church

In the Roman Catholic Church Christians believe that the sacrifice of Jesus for the forgiveness of sins is represented in the sacrament. The chalice may not be given at all services.

The Anglican Church

At the Communion service in the Anglican Church (Church of England) the people come before the altar or Communion table and receive first bread and then wine from a single chalice (or cup).

The Eucharist – A Special Meal

Many religions celebrate special times through the sharing of food. Sometimes the food is the symbol of belief or a sacred meal. For children at the early stages of religious development, it is important to explore the themes which underpin religious belief and practice. One such theme of the Eucharist is 'remembrance'.

Objectives

• To develop an awareness of symbolism in Christianity

Eucharist
Key Stage

KNOWLEDGE AND UNDERSTANDING OF CHRISTIANITY (including belief and practice)
The Church as a Christian community.
Keeping Sunday as a holy day.
The importance of special times to the Christian community.
Worshipping together: reading the Bible; listening to stories; praying.
Special leaders, e.g. priests, ministers, elders.
Christian values: Jesus' teaching on forgiveness and love; relationships with family and friends.
Different names for the sacred meal: Eucharist; Holy Communion; Lord's Supper; Holy Liturgy; Mass; Breaking Bread.

LEARNING EXPERIENCES
Pupils could:
Look at and handle artefacts which are used in Christian worship.
Bake bread and share it with friends.
Share feelings about values which might be important to them, e.g. forgiveness, kindness, loyalty.
Talk about important figures in their own lives.
Write a 'thank you' prayer, a 'sorry' prayer, prayers for ourselves and other people.
Visit a church and learn the names of the key features, e.g. altar/table, pulpit, lectern.
Listen to music associated with a sung Eucharist.

KEY IDEAS AND QUESTIONS ARISING FROM HUMAN EXPERIENCE
Pupils should be encouraged to think about:
What it is like to belong to a group.
How we remember people when we are separated from them.
People who set an example.
How we say 'sorry'.
Meals and celebrations which are special to them.
Books and other objects at home which are special or have special significance.

SYMBOLS
Bread.
Wine.
Cross/crucifix.
Chalice/cup.
Altar/table.
Candles.
Bible.
Prayer-book/order of service/missal.
Liturgical colours.
Water.

Scheme of Work: Eucharist

- To reflect on the importance of 'remembrance' in everyday life
- To develop an awareness of the importance of shared meals

Resources

- A large circular coloured cloth with a small white cloth placed in the centre
- Several prayer books or different orders of service for the Eucharist
- A large Bible (a family Bible is ideal)
- A chalice or goblet for wine
- Bread (of any kind made by the children) or communion wafers bought from a church suppliers
- Two candles and candle sticks
- A bunch of grapes
- A cross or crucifix
- A handkerchief
- A photograph of someone who is special to the teacher
- A calendar or diary
- A recording of sung Eucharist music

Before the activity

Arrange for children to either bring a photograph of an important event in their lives or to paint a picture of a special time.

Setting the scene

Place the large cloth on the floor, putting the smaller cloth in the centre. Display the bread, wine, grapes, chalice, candles and larger Bible on the centre cloth. Place the remaining artefacts on the larger cloth.

26

The activity

Seat the children around the outside of the display.

Invite one child to help light the candles.

Explain the theme of the activity is 'remembering' and comment that we all need to be reminded of events and special times and people, especially when we are separated by time or distance. Tie a knot in the handkerchief and ask if anyone knows why this might be done. Encourage answers like 'to help you remember something important'. Hold up the photograph and comment that it is a 'special' reminder of someone who is not present.

Explain that a diary or a calendar is an important part of school organisation because there are lots of things for teachers to remember which need to be written down. Share the children's photographs or paintings and explain why the times were important.

Explain that Jesus wanted his friends to remember his teaching and a meal they had shared. Christians remember Jesus through sharing a special meal of bread and wine.

Taste the bread or the wafers and end the activity by blowing out the candles.

Sensory learning experiences

Using the display described in the Activities for the Eucharist, which is also illustrated in the drawing, pupils might be encouraged to participate in learning experiences and to explore Christian artefacts.

- Feel the cover of the family Bible.
- Smell the musty smell of an old book.
- Carefully put the ribbon marker in a special page of the Bible.
- Trace the shape of the cross with your fingers.
- Knead dough and make a little cottage loaf.
- Smell the warm dough cooking. Taste warm bread.
- Pour wine (or juice!) from a jug into a chalice or a goblet.
- Put a grape in your mouth and explore the shape with your tongue before you bite it.
- Watch dancing candle flames.
- Listen to sacred Christian music.

Light

Themes of Light occur in many religions. Light and darkness are powerful natural forces, and it is not by accident that festivals often take place either at the darkest or the lightest time of the year.

In the major religions of the world, light is representative of:

- hope
- new life
- separation
- remembrance
- good over evil
- service/dedication
- celebration
- devotion.

In order that pupils increase their understanding of the symbolism of light in worship and religious practice, it is suggested that the first activity might introduce the theme within Christianity, and the second explore light in Judaism. Although each activity focuses on just one of the many celebrations where candles are used, the teacher's notes should provide sufficient information to plan a series of activities based on the same theme.

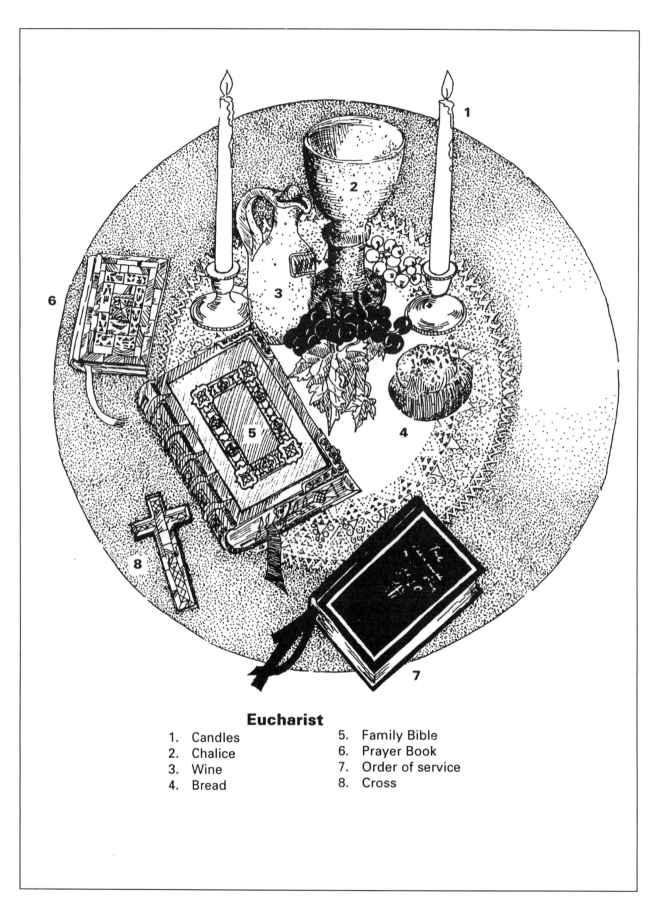

Eucharist

1. Candles
2. Chalice
3. Wine
4. Bread
5. Family Bible
6. Prayer Book
7. Order of service
8. Cross

28

Christian Candles

The symbol of light is often used in Catholic, Anglican and Orthodox churches. Candles are traditionally blessed on Candlemas Day, 2 February. For Christians, candles are a symbol that Jesus is the Light of the World. Special kinds of candles are used during festivals and celebrations and in daily/weekly worship.

Advent candle

Advent candles are used during the four weeks of preparation before the festival of Christmas. Advent candles are marked, and one portion is burnt for each day in Advent. For Christians, the lighting of Advent candles symbolises the coming of the Christ-child.

Some churches have Advent rings: four candles in a circle of evergreen. One candle is lit each Sunday in Advent. A fifth candle in the centre is lit on Christmas Day.

Paschal candle (Easter)

In some churches an Easter vigil is kept the night before the festival. The building remains in darkness until the Easter fire is kindled. A large paschal candle is lit from the Easter fire, and the light is passed to each member of the congregation so that s/he may light an individual candle.

Symbols on the paschal candle include:

- the chi-rho, the first two letters of Christ's name in Greek
- alpha and omega, the first and last letters of the Greek alphabet, a symbol that Jesus is the beginning and the end of all things as quoted in the book of Revelation 21:6: 'He said to me, "Write this, because these words are true and can be trusted." And he said, "I am the first and the last, the beginning and the end."' (Good News Bible)
- the sleeping Roman guards at the tomb of Jesus
- the year in which the candle is to be used
- doves which represent the Holy Spirit and peace
- a laurel crown replacing the crown of thorns and representing the kingship of Jesus
- studs of incense, symbolic of the suffering of Jesus.

TO MAKE A CHRISTINGLE

You will need:
A sharp knife
An orange
A candle
20 cms of thin red parcel ribbon
Cocktail sticks
Raisins and sweets (Jelly Tots or Dolly Mixtures are ideal)
Pins

1. With a knife, cut a cross in the top of the orange.
2. Press the candle into the hole.
3. Thread the fruit and the sweets on to the cocktail sticks and push them into the orange.
4. Put the red ribbon around the orange and hold it on with the pins. Tie the ribbon in a bow.
5. Light the candle and explain that it is a symbol of the arrival of the Christ child as the Light of the World.

Baptismal candle

This is given to a child at baptism with the words, 'Receive this light. This is to show that you have passed from darkness to light.' The candle may be lit each year on the anniversary of the baptism or on the child's birthday.

Votive candle

In some churches, votive candles are placed by worshippers near to a statue of a saint or an icon in the hope that the saint will continue to intervene on behalf of the worshipper after they have left the place of worship. Sometimes a stand holds votive candles, placed as a sign that a 'special' prayer has been offered.

Christingle

One of the traditional celebrations of Advent in England is a Christingle service in Church. The children of the congregation are given a candle in an orange, which is decorated with fruit, sweets and a red ribbon.

- The orange represents the World.

- The candle represents Jesus, the Light of the World.
- The red ribbon represents the blood of Jesus.
- The sticks represent the four seasons or the four corners of the earth.
- The fruit represents the fruits of the earth.

Objectives

- To help children explore experiences of light and darkness in daily life
- To help children to begin to understand the symbolism of light and darkness in the Christian religious tradition.

Resources

- A large circular tablecloth
- A birthday cake with several candles
- A collection of artefacts or symbols symbolic of Advent/Christmas, e.g. nativity figures; Advent calendar; holly
- A collection of Advent candles and a variety of decorative ones in different shapes, colours and sizes, displayed attractively
- Items required to make a Christingle (see above)
- Matches
- A tape of music which is representative of the theme of light/darkness, e.g. Zanfir – Pan Pipes; Light of Experience
- A room which can be darkened

Setting the scene

Arrange the display, lighting one or two of the candles which will not be passed around. Play the tape of music and ask the children to focus their attention on the candle flames.

The activity

Light the birthday cake candles and explain that the theme of the activity is light. Why do we put candles on birthday cakes? Expect the answer, 'To show us how old someone is'! Ask, 'How do candles make you feel?'

Explain that just as families at home use birthday candles as a symbol of a special occasion, so does the Christian family in church. Introduce the various candles and pass unlit examples around for the children to touch and to look at closely. Explain that during Advent, Christians sometimes attend a special celebration in church called a Christingle service.

Demonstrate how a Christingle is made. For more able children, explore the possible symbolism of the various features of the Christingle as they are arranged on the orange. Darken the room, light the Christingle and ask the children to think about someone who is very special to them as they listen once again to the music.

2. Jewish Candles

Themes of light and darkness are common in Judaism and candles are used for devotion, celebration and as memorials.

Shabbat candles (Sabbath)

Two candles are lit in Jewish homes on Friday before sunset, the eve of the Sabbath. The woman of the house recites a special blessing before they are lit and repeats the words Shabbat Shalom ('A peaceful Shabbat').

The light is a symbol of the goodness and joy of the occasion. The candlesticks are often silver, and they may be family heirlooms, passed down from one generation to the next.

Havdalah candle

The Havdalah candle has several wicks in order to give a lot of light. The name Havdalah means 'separate'. In other words, the Sabbath is unlike the working days of the week. The candle is lit at the Havdalah service which marks the end of the Sabbath. Members of the family stretch out their hands towards the candle, a symbol of bringing together the joy and celebration of the occasion.

Shabbat
Key Stage

KNOWLEDGE AND UNDERSTANDING OF JUDAISM (including belief and practice)

Israel as a special place for Jewish families.
Family and community life.
Responsibility to God: the Shema; mezuzah; tallit; kippah; the Ten Commandments.
Special places: the Synagogue.
Special times: Shabbat and the Friday night meal; Pesach.
Stories and guidance in the Torah.

LEARNING EXPERIENCES

Pupils could:

Watch and listen to a Jewish family preparing for Shabbat and explore the symbolism involved, e.g. lighting candles, blessing the children, blessing the wine, eating as a family.
Join in a Sabbath meal and share experiences of celebrations they enjoy.
Share any prayers which are special to them with the rest of the class.
Share feelings about the importance of family and friends.
Talk about special times and occasions in their own lives.
Listen to passages from the Torah or songs and psalms associated with Shabbat.
Cook (and/or) eat Challah bread sprinkled with salt.
Look at and talk about some of the items associated with the Friday night meal, e.g. candles, kiddush cup, spice box.

Visit a Synagogue and learn the names of the key points, e.g. Ner Tamid, The Ark, Torah Scrolls, Bimah.
Design a Synagogue showing the main rooms and key features.

KEY IDEAS AND QUESTIONS ARISING FROM HUMAN EXPERIENCE

Pupils should be encouraged to think about:
Homes that they know.
People who care for them.
What is important in their own lives.
Special occasions and places in their own lives.

SYMBOLS

Challah.
Kiddush cup.
Shabbat manual.
Candles (including Havdalah).
Wine.
Spice box.
Tallit.
Kippah.
Menorah.

Scheme of Work: Shabbat

Hanukkah candles

A Hanukiah is a candlestick with eight or nine branches which is used during Hanukkah, the festival of lights. Hanukkah is celebrated to remind Jews of the bravery of a small group of people who fought for their faith against a pagan emperor (see story below). On the first evening of the festival, as soon as three stars can be seen in the sky, a candle is lit from the centre servant or 'shamash' candle. An additional candle is kindled each night of the festival. The lighting of the candles is followed by reading the following verse from the prayer book:

> ...these lights are holy and we are not permitted to make use of them, but only to see them in order to thank your name for the wonders, the victories and the marvellous deeds.

THE HANUKKAH STORY

Hanukkah is a Jewish festival of light which occurs in November or December. The festival remembers the victory of Judah the Maccabee over the Syrians, who had forbidden the Jews to worship their God and had put idols in their temple. When the Jews had overcome the Syrians, the first thing they did was to restore the temple. Some people think that this took eight days.
The Syrians had stolen the oil which was used to keep the temple lamp burning and the Jews searched for a long time until they found a very tiny amount – just enough to keep the lamp alight for one day. But a miracle was worked, and the lamp stayed alight for eight days. So Jewish people remember the occasion by celebrating Hanukkah as an eight-day festival.

Memorial candle

On the anniversary of a death, the family of the deceased will often light a memorial candle as a sign of remembrance.

THE SABBATH TABLE

Two challah loaves, a kiddush cup
And candles burning bright
Make my home a special place
Every Friday night.

The Shabbat table is like a princess
Like a princess dressed in white
Who wears a crown of candles
Candles sparkling bright.

(Written by year 6 pupils, Stapleford School)

OUR CHALLAH LOAVES

We have two challah loaves
We made them ourselves
We baked them in the oven
We put them on the shelves.

We have two challah loaves
We took them from the shelves
We put them on the table
And covered them ourselves.

We have two Shabbat candles
On the table burning bright
And now we say a special prayer
'Shabbat Shallom', tonight.

(Erica Brown)

DEUTERONOMY 5:12

Remember the Sabbath and keep it holy. You have six days in which to work, but the seventh day is the day of rest. On the Sabbath day no one is to work – not you or your children or your servants, your animals or anyone who is visiting you.

PRAYER RECITED WHEN LIGHTING SHABBAT CANDLES
The woman of the house lights the candles saying:
O God you have made the Sabbath and the people of Israel holy. You have called upon us to honour the Sabbath with light, with joy, with peace...may the light of the candles drive out anger from within us...may my children walk in the ways of Your Truth, Your Light.

Objectives
- To help children explore experiences of light and darkness in daily life
- To help children to begin to understand the symbolism of light and darkness in the Jewish tradition

Resources
A table or a large circular tablecloth set with the following:

- a clean white cloth
- a place-setting of fine china
- two candlesticks with candles
- a kiddush cup (wine goblet)
- two challot (plaited loaves)
- prayer-book
- phylacteries (small pieces of parchment inscribed with passages from scripture, worn in a box on the left arm or forehead and bound to the body with leather straps)
- a copy of Deuteronomy 5:12
- matches
- copy of the prayer of blessing recited by the woman of the house
- a room which can be darkened
- copy of the poems 'The Shabbat Table' and 'Our Challot Loaves'

Setting the scene

Set up the display and include other Jewish artefacts if they are readily available.

The activity

Ask the children if they can remember any of the times when special candles are used by Christians. Explain that Jews also use the symbol of light in worship and for special occasions.

Invite children to think of the kinds of things which they use to set the table at home for a special occasion.

Introduce the theme of Shabbat as a 'special time' and read Deuteronomy 5:12.

Comment on the format of the table-setting, paying particular attention to the candles.

Invite one child to help light the Shabbat candles and explain that the meal cannot begin until the 'mother' of a household has recited a special blessing over her family.

CHALLAH BREAD

Challah is a plaited loaf. Two challot are served at each of the three Sabbath meals and eaten sprinkled with salt. The loaves are kept covered by a cloth until they are ready to eat. The three strands of the plaits are symbolic of the relationship between God, Torah (Teaching) and the people of Israel.

25g easy-mix yeast
1 tsp. sugar
200g plain white flour
1 tsp. salt
2 tbsps vegetable oil
1 egg
3 tsp. poppy seeds
beaten egg to glaze

1. Mix the yeast with the sugar and two tablespoons of warm water. Leave until frothy (5-10 minutes).
2. Mix the flour and the salt together.
3. Make a well in the centre of the flour, and add the egg, the yeast mixture and enough water to make a stiff dough.
4. Beat the dough very thoroughly.
5. Turn the dough out on to a board and knead for 5 minutes.
6. Divide the dough into six pieces, knead each piece and roll into long 'sausage' shapes.
7. Take three strands of dough, squeeze together at one end and then plait the pieces together, squeezing together firmly at the finished end also.
8. Repeat with the remaining dough 'sausages'.
9. Place the loaves on to a greased baking tray and sprinkle with water.
10. Place the loaves into two polythene bags greased with vegetable oil and set aside in a warm place until they have doubled in size (about an hour).
11. Remove the loaves from the bags, brush with beaten egg and sprinkle with poppy seeds.
12. Bake for about 10 minutes in a pre-heated oven at 200°C/400°F and then reduce the heat to 150°C/350°F for 45 minutes.

Shabbat

1. Shabbat candles
2. Spice box
3. Phylacteries
4. Challah loaves
5. Kippah
6. Miniature Torah scroll & case
7. Yad
8. Tallit
9. Havdalah candle
10. Kiddush cup

Pass around Havdalah candles for children to hold, allowing time for them to trace the plaits with their fingers.

Comment that just as Shabbat begins with lighting candles, so it ends the same way, but that the several wicks on the Havdalah candle burn very brightly to remind Jews that the Sabbath is a special day set apart from the other days of the week.

End the activity by darkening the room so that it is lit only by the candles and asking each child to break off a small portion from the challah bread. Ask them to give the bread to the person on his/her right-hand side. Each person must eat the piece of bread given to them before breaking off a piece for the next person. More able children might repeat the words, 'Shabbat Shalom' (a peaceful Sabbath).

Sensory learning experiences

Using the display described in the Activities for Jewish Candles, which is also illustrated in the drawing, pupils might be encouraged to explore Jewish artefacts.

- Enjoy the sparkling whiteness of the starched cloth.
- Knead the **challah** dough and roll it into 'sausage' shapes .
- Sprinkle poppy seeds.
- Plait the dough 'sausages'.
- Smell the warm bread cooking.
- Hold the **Torah** scroll and ask a friend to very carefully point to some letters with the **yad**.
- Enjoy feeling the texture of the velvet Torah scroll case.
- Wear a **capel** and see how you look in a mirror.
- Wear a **tallit** and enjoy the texture of the cool silk against your neck and the 'tickly' feel of the fringes on your arms.
- Trace the plaits of the **havdalah** candle with your fingers.
- Feel the row of cotton wicks along the top of the **havdalah** candle.
- Watch the big flame of the **havdalah** candle.
- Put the **havdalah** candle in the holder.
- Feel the warmth of the candle flames.
- Blow out the candle flames.
- Smell the cinnamon, cloves and nutmeg in the **spice box**.
- Smell the leather of the phylacteries.

The Seder (Passover) Meal

The Seder meal is more than an ordinary family meal. It is a religious 'drama' which needs special preparation, not only by those who cook the food and conduct the service, but by those who share it. Traditionally there are fifteen steps in the meal, corresponding, it is said, to the steps leading up to the Holy of Holies of the ancient temple in Jerusalem.

The setting of the table has become a symbolic feature of the Passover (Pesach) meal. Each Seder meal will include the following:

Seder plate

The Seder dish holds the symbolic foods which are eaten during the Passover meal. There are many different styles of Seder plates and often they are family heirlooms handed down from generation to generation.

Candles

The beginning of the Seder meal is marked by a blessing and the lighting of two candles. Candlesticks are often family heirlooms.

Z'roah (shank bone)

This is a reminder of the sacrifice of the paschal lamb once offered in the temple on Mount Zion and then consumed together with bitter herbs and unleavened bread. Today a bone is roasted but lamb is not eaten.

Egg

A roasted egg is a symbol of the lamb which was once offered by the Israelites as a part of sacrificial worship in the temple. An egg is also a symbol of the renewal of life in the springtime.

Charoset

A mortar-like paste made from apples, cinnamon, wine, etc (see recipe), which is representative of the bricks which the Israelites used for building when they were in slavery. It is eaten with maror and also with matzot (see Numbers 9: 11).

CHAROSET

Charoset is eaten at the Seder meal. It is a mortar-like paste, symbolic of the cement used to build the pyramids when the Israelites were in captivity in Egypt. It tastes much better than it looks!

1 large cooking apple	1. Peel and core the apple.
100g walnuts	2. Mince the walnuts and apple in a food processor.
2 level tsp. cinnamon	3. Place the nuts and the apple into a mixing bowl.
2 level dtsp. clear honey	4. Add the cinnamon and the honey.
a little white wine or	5. Moisten with wine or grape juice and mix together.
grape juice	

Karpas (parsley)

Parsley is a symbol of spring and new life. It is eaten dipped in salt water which represents the tears of the Israelites when they were in captivity.

Maror (horseradish)

Maror is symbolic of the lives of the Israelites which were embittered by suffering in Egypt. Maror is dipped into the charoset and eaten (see Exodus 1: 14).

Three matzot

Matzot or unleavened bread is eaten as a reminder of the unleavened bread which was baked by the Israelites in their hurry to leave Egypt (see Exodus 12: 39). The matzot will be either contained within separate compartments of a matzot cover or separated from one another by the folds of a napkin.

Elijah's cup

The prophet Malachi promised that Elijah would return to announce the coming of the Messiah. Traditionally a place is always set for the prophet Elijah at the Seder table, and the door of the house is opened to welcome him should he arrive.

Wine

Four goblets of wine are consumed by each person at the meal. The story of the ten plagues which God sent to force the Egyptians to release the Israelites is told, and one drop of wine for each plague is spilled. Wine is a symbol of joy, and even though the Egyptians were the enemies of the Israelites, their downfall should be remembered with compassion.

Hagadah

The narration of the Seder meal is found in the Hagadah, and this book will be used at all Passover meals.

For pupils to understand Passover, they need to be familiar with shared meals for special occasions. It is also best if they have heard the Exodus story and are able to help with the preparation of the food on the Seder plate. The activity is best for a small group of children.

Objectives

- To encourage the children to reflect on their own experience of celebration – at home, school and in the wider community
- To develop an awareness of how religious beliefs and insights are expressed in symbolism
- To develop an awareness of the events within a community which are significant to its people

Resources

- A large circular tablecloth
- A Seder plate

PESACH
Key Stage

KNOWLEDGE AND UNDERSTANDING OF JUDAISM
(including belief and practice)
Israel as a special place for Jewish families.
Family and community life.
Responsibility to God: the Shema; mezuzah; tallit;
kippah; the Ten Commandments.
The Synagogue.
Special times: Shabbat Pesach; Sukkot.
The Exodus story.

LEARNING EXPERIENCES
Pupils could:
Listen to the story of the Exodus.
Discover how people express their identity.
Share feeling about the importance of families and
friends.
Visit a Synagogue or watch a video showing the key
features in a Synagogue.
Find Israel and Jerusalem on a globe or in an atlas.
Plan, shop for and prepare a Seder meal.
Identify and arrange the symbolic foods on a Seder plate.
Examine a mezuzah and its contents and talk about why it
is important.

KEY IDEAS AND QUESTIONS ARISING FROM
HUMAN EXPERIENCE
Pupils should be encouraged to think about:
  What is important or special to them.
    Special times of the year.
      People who are less fortunate – especially those
      who, for whatever reasons, are unable to be with
      family and friends
      The importance of doing things together.

SYMBOLS
    Seder plate.
    Shank bone.
    Roasted egg.
    Charoset.
    Parsley.
    Horse radish or bitter herbs.
    Lettuce.
    Matzot.
    Elijah's cup.
    Hagadah.

Scheme of Work: Pesach

- Passover (Pesach) paper napkins and greetings cards (if possible)
- Miniature Torah scrolls
- Yad (a pointer used in reading the scrolls)
- Prayer hats (Kippah)
- Candles and candlesticks
- Lamb bone
- Roasted egg (hard-boiled and held over a flame to burn the shell)
- Lettuce
- A bunch of parsley
- Charoset (see recipe)
- Horseradish (either a small piece of root or a jar of relish)
- Three matzot (bought in the red packet, marked, 'For Passover Use' covered with a matzot cover
- Goblets of wine (or substitute!)
- Hagadah
- Salt water in small dishes
- Matches
- A copy of 'The Exodus Story'.

Setting the scene

Place the tablecloth on the floor with the Seder plate in the centre. Arrange the napkins, greetings cards, Torah scrolls, Hagadah, yad, prayer hats, candles and candlesticks, matzot and salt water on the cloth. Have the other items close to hand. Light the candles.

The activity

Seat the group of children around the cloth and 'set the scene' by inviting a child to light the candles. Ask whether anyone knows what is special about the display. Why is it laid out as if for a meal on a table?

Explain that the Passover meal celebrates freedom from slavery and retell the Exodus story briefly.

Ask one child to read or sign the question, 'Why is this night different from all other nights?' Four other children might read or sign the replies.

Pesach

1. Candles
2. Hagadah
3. Pesach cards
4. Kosher wine
5. Elijah's cup
6. Kippah
7. Matzot and matzot cover
8. Seder plate
9. Miniature Torah scroll and yad

THE FOUR QUESTIONS

For the Jewish people, the festival of Passover celebrates freedom from slavery.

'Why is this night different from all other nights?' the child asks during the Seder meal.

In reply he is told, 'On all other nights we eat both leavened and unleavened bread, but tonight only unleavened bread.'

'On all other nights we eat any herbs we wish, but tonight only bitter herbs.'

'On all other nights we need not dip any food at all, but tonight we dip twice.'

'On all other nights we eat sitting or reclining, but tonight we all recline.'

Hold up the Seder plate and, taking each symbol in turn, explain its significance and place it in the appropriate place on the plate (most Seder plates will have symbols or words on them).

Pass around the parsley and dip a small piece in salt water. Invite children to eat it. Explain again the symbolism of the salt water (tears) and parsley (new life).

Uncover the matzot and hand it round, inviting each child to break off a small piece to dip in the charoset to eat.

End the activity by asking the pupils to focus on the candle flames. Blow out the candle.

Sensory learning experiences

Using the display which is illustrated in the drawing, pupils might be encouraged to participate in learning experiences and to explore Jewish artefacts.

- Put the candles in the holders.
- Enjoy the tactile qualities of the **Seder** plate.
- Wear a **capel** and see how it looks in a mirror.
- Help to put **matzot** in the folds of the **matzot** cover.
- Pour wine (or juice) into **Elijah's** cup.
- Pick spring flowers and put them in a vase.
- Smell the flowers.
- Discover how the **hagadah** opens.
- Hard boil an egg and smell the singed aroma as it is held with cooking tongs by a grown up over a flame.
- Chew lettuce and discover how it tastes sweet at first and then bitter.
- Dip a sprig of parsley in salt water and eat it.
- Help to grate apple for **charoset.**
- Mix the charoset ingredients and taste some on a piece of matzah.
- Discover the shape of the **yad** like a tiny hand with a finger to point to the words on the **Torah scroll.**

Guru Nanak's Birthday

Guru Nanak was the founder of Sikhism. The word Sikh means 'disciple'. Guru Nanak was born a Hindu but he rejected the caste system and idolatry and he taught that only one God should be worshipped.

Guru Nanak is deeply admired by Sikhs as an example of piety and holiness. He is regarded as a man who was chosen by God to reveal His message.

The celebration of Guru Nanak's birthday is universal in Sikhism. Guru Nanak was born in April, but his birthday is celebrated in November each year. The original reason for this was probably linked with the Hindu Festival of Divali where the main symbolism is that of light overcoming darkness. It seems likely that early Sikhs saw November as a good time in which to celebrate the birthday of their Guru who *enlightened* them in the ways of God.

The preparations for the festival are extremely important and they form part of the festival itself. Men ensure that they are wearing the five symbols of Sikhism: **kesh** (uncut hair), **kangha** (comb to hold kesh in place), **kara** (bangle), **kachera** (underwear), **kirpan** (sword). Women wear traditional Punjabi dress in the homeland (often a

Guru Nanak's Birthday
Key Stage

KNOWLEDGE AND UNDERSTANDING OF SIKHISM
(including belief and practice)
There is one God who is the Creator.
All humans are equal before God.
Ceremonies: e.g. naming, marriage, turban-tying.
Celebrations: e.g. birthdays of Guru Nanak, Guru Gobind Singh: Baisakhi.
The lives of the Gurus.
The Guru Granth Sahib – its care in the Gurdwara.
Worship – led by the Granthi. Consists of: kirtan; ardas; langar.

LEARNING EXPERIENCES
Pupils could:
Hear Sikhs talking about themselves and their faith.
Listen to stories about Guru Nanak and other Gurus.
Observe a Sikh tying his turban.
Find out about the birthday of Guru Nanak and how it is celebrated.
Look at pictures or a video of the Golden temple and find out where Amritsar is on a map.
Listen to the story of Baisakhi.
Share ideas about the importance of the names and look up their own names in a dictionary of first names.
Visit a Gurdwara and identify expressions of Sikh belief and practice.
Make a poster explaining the 5 Ks.
Design their own symbol(s) to express something about themselves.

KEY IDEAS AND QUESTIONS ARISING FROM HUMAN EXPERIENCE
Pupils should be encouraged to think about:
Times when it is easy to share and times when it is difficult.
Their own families and the activities which they enjoy.
Signs of belonging, e.g. uniforms, badges, symbols.
Ways in which people demonstrate respect, and how it feels to be respected.
Feelings which are evoked when visiting a place of worship.
The importance of community meals – meals which are special.
Books which are special to them.

SYMBOLS
The 5 Ks: kachera; kangha; kara; kesh; kirpan.
Karah parshad.
Khanda.
Nishan Sahib.

Scheme of Work: Guru Nanak's Birthday

sari, or tunic over trousers and a scarf on their head) and many will find ornamental ways of wearing some, if not all, of the five symbols.

Two days before the birthday a complete reading of the **Guru Granth Sahib** (Holy Book) begins, with members of the community sharing the task of chanting or reciting it continuously throughout the day and night. A ceremonial meal is prepared in the temple kitchen (**langar**) during the reading of the Guru Granth Sahib. This is called **karah parshad**.

Hymns are recited while the preparations are taking place. The karah parshad is covered with a clean cloth and taken into the Gurdwara and placed near the **Granthi**. After the prayer of **Ardas** (petition) the karah parshad is cut with a two-edged sword and each person present is given a small piece as a symbol of unity and brotherhood.

Later in the day, a procession takes place, and, in Punjab, the Guru Granth Sahib is paraded through the streets on a raised seat or throne, often with a canopy overhead and accompanied by a guard of honour of five men. These men represent the first five members of the Khalsa who were prepared to die for the brotherhood. Each member of the bodyguard carries a richly decorated kirpan. Members of the congregation accompany the procession singing, chanting and scattering flower petals. At times the procession is halted so guest speakers may read or tell stories about the life and teaching of Guru Nanak. When the speaker has finished the crowd shout 'Waheguru', meaning 'wonderful Guru'.

In Amritsar there are great celebrations for Guru Nanak's birthday. At the Golden Temple, hundreds of small ghee lamps are lit around the perimeter of the sacred pool which surrounds the building and the Guru Granth Sahib is processed in the streets.

In Britain the festival is usually celebrated in the Gurdwara with parties at home afterwards.

Objectives

• To help pupils reflect on celebrations and occasions which occur annually

A STORY FROM GURU NANAK
THE NEEDLE STORY

Guru Nanak used to travel from village to village along dusty roads of India. One day he came to a town and saw a house decorated with dozens of flags. The local people told him that the man who lived there was very rich and every time he acquired a thousand rupees he flew another flag. 'This man needs some guidance,' said Guru Nanak. 'He has got it all wrong. Money is no use unless you use it to help other people.'

He went to see the man, who was called Duni Chand, and gave him a needle. 'Look after this needle and give it back to me when we meet in the next world,' he said.

Duni Chand took the needle back to his wife. 'This man must be mad,' he said. They both decided to go back to the Guru and return his needle. 'We can't do it,' they told Guru Nanak. 'We can't take anything with us into the next world.'

Guru Nanak smiled and asked them, 'Why are you saving up all this money then?' The couple looked shocked – they had not thought of that before. 'There is only one thing you can take into the next world,' he told them, 'the kindness you have done in this life.'

Duni Chand learned his lesson. He did not give up his business in Lahore but he did use all his money to help the poorer people who lived near him.

KARAH PARSHAD

Karah Parshad is shared by worshippers and visitors in a gurdwara. It is eaten with the fingers.

100g unsalted butter
50g plain flour
100g semolina or ground rice
100g sugar and 425 ml water boiled together

1. Melt the butter in a saucepan and add the flour, beating well with a wooden spoon over a very gentle heat.
2. Add the semolina or ground rice, continuing to beat well.
3. Heat until the butter separates.
4. Remove from the heat and add the sugared water very gradually, stirring until a stiff paste is formed.
5. Cool slightly before eating.

- To develop an awareness of how religious beliefs and lifestyles are expressed through symbolism
- To increase pupils' knowledge and experience of stories about key figures and leaders in religion.

Resources
- A large brightly coloured circular tablecloth
- A collection of Sikh artefacts including a framed picture of Guru Nanak and the 5 Ks
- A Sikh garland used for decoration
- The Needle Story (see above)
- Divas or nightlights contained in brightly coloured holders
- A small amount of karah parshad (see recipe)
- Examples of symbols, badges, special clothes which are familiar to the pupils and representative of groups to which they belong.

Setting the scene
Invite several pupils to help put the tablecloth on the floor. Seat the group around the edge of the empty cloth.

Have examples of symbols and badges which are familiar to the pupils and a box of carefully wrapped Sikh artefacts close to hand.

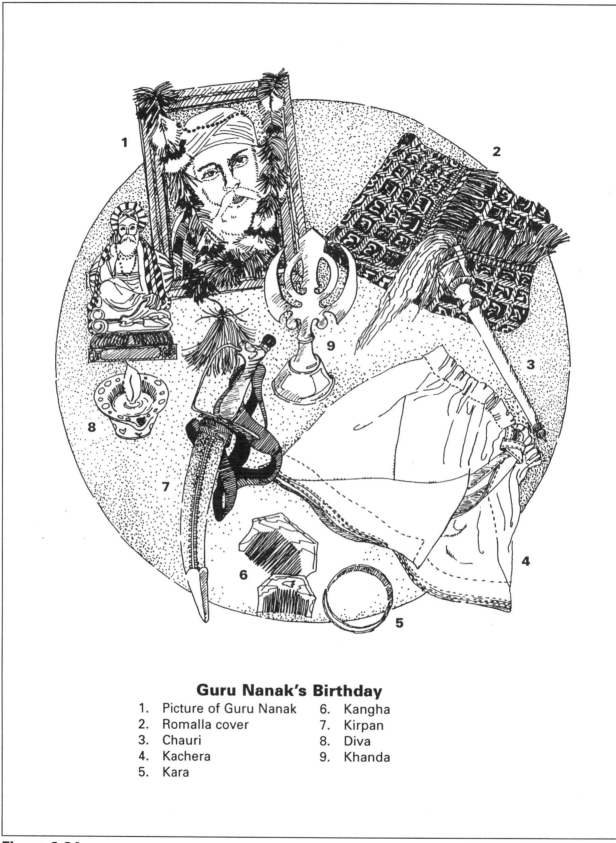

Guru Nanak's Birthday

1. Picture of Guru Nanak
2. Romalla cover
3. Chauri
4. Kachera
5. Kara
6. Kangha
7. Kirpan
8. Diva
9. Khanda

Figure 6.24

The activity

Talk about the symbols, badges, clothing etc which belong to the pupils, emphasising how important they are because they are representative of special places, groups etc. Invite pupils to place their symbols on one half of the cloth.

Introduce the 5 Ks by very carefully unwrapping them and explaining they are symbols which Sikh people use to show they belong to the faith. (Be careful with the kirpan if it is sharp). Allow pupils to try on the kara and to feel the tactile quality of the wooden comb. Display the 5Ks on the other half of the cloth and once again draw the attention of group members to their symbols.

Carefully unwrap the picture of Guru Nanak and talk about 'special' people and leaders within the pupils' experience. Explain that Guru Nanak is a special person for Sikh people and place the picture on the cloth close to the 5Ks.

Ask how the pupils celebrate their birthdays. Encourage discussion about cakes and shared meals with families and friends.

Tell the Needle Story and explain how Sikh people celebrate Guru Nanak's birthday. Invite a pupil to decorate the picture of Guru Nanak with the garland. Place a lighted diva on the cloth, emphasising how important candles and light are for festivals and celebrations. Share small portions of karah parshad.

At the end of the activity, pack the Sikh artefacts away, reminding pupils of the importance of looking after 'special' objects.

Sensory learning experiences

Using the display described in the Activities for Guru Nanak's birthday, which is also illustrated in the drawing, pupils might be encouraged to explore Sikh artefacts.

- Trace the shape of the **khanda** with your fingers.
- Touch the coarse yak hair of the **chauri.**
- Feel the tactile qualities of the wooden **kangha.**
- Put the **garland** over your head and look at your image in a mirror.
- Wear the **kara.** Feel the coolness of the steel and its weight on your wrist.
- Smell warm **karah parshad.**
- Smell the candle wax of the **diva.**
- Watch the curving diva flame.
- Taste warm **karah parshad.**
- Look at the rich embroidery on the **romalla** cover.
- Feel the fringes of the romalla cover against your face.

Id-ul-Fitr

The fast of Ramadan ends with the three day festival of 'Breaking the Fast', on the first day of the following month. It is known as Id-ul-Fitr and is a time for rejoicing in God's favour.

Id-ul-Fitr is also a festival of alms-giving when those Muslims who have not paid zakah (a charitable contribution) during Ramadan are able to do so.

Id-ul-Fitr is a time for giving gifts. Most Muslims will bathe and put on new or best clothes. The festival begins at the mosque about an hour after sunset and the night of Id-ul-Fitr is traditionally spent in meditation and prayer. There are many traditions associated with Id-ul-Fitr, but most are based on the Five Pillars of Islam, together with thanksgiving for a successful fast during Ramadan.

Objectives

- To develop an awareness of the events within the Muslim community which are significant to its people
- To develop an awareness of the diversity of human response to life.
- To develop an understanding of how religious beliefs and insights are expressed through symbolism
- To reflect on family customs and traditions in their own homes and special occasions which occur annually
- To encourage an ability to share with others, nurturing attitudes of tolerance and respect

Resources

- A large circular tablecloth and a smaller cloth

ID-UL-FITR
Key Stage

**KNOWLEDGE AND UNDERSTANDING OF ISLAM
(including belief and practice)**
The Oneness of Allah.
Allah has sent guidance through the Qur'an and the Prophets.
Muslims serve Allah in many ways including daily prayer.
Homes and family life.
Stories from the life and traditions of the Prophet Muhammad.
The role of the Mosque
The importance of special times to the Muslim community.
Preparing for festivals and special times.
The importance of self-discipline.

LEARNING EXPERIENCES
Pupils could:
Observe wudu and salah and find out where and how they take place.
Learn that the Islamic name for God is 'Allah'.
Join in the celebration of Id-ul-Fitr and share experiences of celebrations they enjoy.
Give and receive gifts.
Listen to passages read from the Qur'an and listen to stories about the life of Muhammad.
Dress dolls and dress up in shalwar, kameez, topi.
Listen to Muslims talking about Hajj.
Visit a Mosque.
Find out about how different people express their beliefs through symbols, stories, language.

Share feelings about gratitude and thankfulness.
Share fresh dates.

KEY IDEAS AND QUESTIONS ARISING FROM HUMAN EXPERIENCE
Pupils should be encouraged to think about:
Why some books are very special.
How and why we have celebrations.
What it must be like to go without food and water all day.
Giving and receiving gifts.
Those who are less fortunate.

SYMBOLS
Signs and symbols in everyday life.
Special foods: dates; water; sweetmeats.
Feasting and fasting.
New moon.

Scheme of Work: Id-ul-Fitr

- A prayer carpet
- A Qur'an stand and a wrapped translation of the Qur'an
- Id-ul-Fitr cards
- A compass
- Several topis
- A bowl large enough for washing hands and soap, water and a towel
- Several story or picture books which are special to the children
- Fresh dates

Setting the scene

Put the tablecloth in the centre of a fairly large space on the floor.
Collect together the artefacts and the water, soap and towel.

The activity

Seat the children around the cloth and invite several to help lay the smaller cloth on top of the larger one. Explain the importance of washing hands and talk about the times when children are asked to wash. Invite everyone present to wash their hands. Carefully unroll the carpet and place it to one side of the display.

Talk about the children's books and discover which way they open. Set up the Qur'an stand. Ask if anyone can guess what is inside the wrapped bundle. Very carefully unwrap it and talk about how special the book is to Muslims. Show the children which way the Qur'an opens and draw their attention to the beautiful calligraphy. Place the open Qur'an on the stand.

Discover which way the greetings cards open and add these to the display together with the other artefacts, commenting as appropriate.

Id-ul-Fitr

1. Prayer carpet
2. Id-ul-Fitr cards
3. Compass
4. Topi
5. Pendant
6. Qur'an and stand

Share fresh dates and save the stones to plant later.

End the activity by asking the children to help put everything away very carefully, paying particular attention to wrapping up the Qur'an.

Sensory learning experiences

Using the display which is illustrated in the drawing, pupils might be encouraged to participate in learning experiences and to explore Muslim artefacts.

- Unroll a prayer carpet and feel the fabric with the palms of your hands.
- Explore the beautiful design of the carpet.
- Help to set up the Qur'an stand.
- Trace the intricate carving of the Qur'an stand with your fingers.
- Wash your hands before you hold the translation of the Qur'an.
- Enjoy the beauty of the Arabic calligraphy.
- Wear a pendant and see how you look in a mirror.
- Wear a topi and see how you look in a mirror.
- Open the compass case and discover the direction of Makkah.

Holi

Holi is a two-day or three-day North Indian Hindu festival which marks the turn of the season from winter to spring. It is celebrated in the month of Phalguna in the Hindu calendar (usually February or March in the Gregorian calendar). The festival takes its name from Holika, a demoness.

The ways in which Holi is celebrated vary, but it is usually a noisy time when caste and class barriers are ignored and everyday lifestyles are abandoned. Celebrations at Holi include the lighting of bonfires and the offering of the first crops of the spring harvest to God, the sharing of food, and the spraying of coloured dyes and powders.

In some villages it is believed that the direction of the flames of the bonfires indicates the most fertile land for the following year. As the flames die down, coconuts are roasted and shared, and pieces of the hot embers may be carried home to kindle domestic Holi fires.

The origins of Holi are obscure although traditional religious stories are retold, such as those about Lord Krishna. In temples, foods like nuts and fruits are offered to God before the celebration begins with a fast and prayers, followed by feasting on dairy products, sweetmeats and vegetarian dishes.

Holi is a festival full of fun and colour. Themes which might be explored in association with the celebration are:

- light
- darkness
- fire
- colours
- harvest
- jokes/pranks
- feasting and fasting.

Objectives

- To develop an awareness of the events within the Hindu community which are significant to its people
- To develop an awareness of the diversity of human response to life
- To develop an understanding of how religious beliefs and insights are expressed in symbolism
- To reflect on family customs and traditions in their own homes and special occasions which occur annually.
- To encourage an ability to share with others, nurturing attitudes of tolerance and respect

Resources

- A large circular tablecloth
- Indian garlands, Hindu artefacts, Indian musical instruments (finger cymbals, bells, drums), divas, coconuts, etc.
- Red, yellow and orange tissue paper
- A few small logs/sticks or Indian lamps
- Joss sticks and holders
- Coloured streamers or confetti

HOLI

Key Stage

KNOWLEDGE AND UNDERSTANDING OF HINDUISM
(including belief and practice)
Devotion to God.
Respect for God, other people and all forms of life.
The community as a family.
Different roles within the community.
Foods associated with Hindu worship and celebration.
God represented in different forms through images.
Stories about Krishna (Puranas).
Names of some of the scriptures and how they are used by adherents.
Worship in the home and at the Mandir.
Love and loyalty between members of the extended family.

LEARNING EXPERIENCES
Pupils could:
Join in a Holi celebration and share experiences of celebrations they enjoy.
Share feelings about the importance of family and friends.
Give and receive gifts.
Find out about life in India.
Listen to stories about Holi and about Krishna.
Look at images of Krishna in pictures and artefacts.
Explore and reflect upon sights, colours, smells, tastes, sounds of Holi celebrations.
Talk about events in their own lives which compare with stories about Krishna.
Dress dolls or dress up in saris/dhotis.
Visit a Mandir.

KEY IDEAS AND QUESTIONS ARISING FROM HUMAN EXPERIENCE
Pupils should be encouraged to think about:
Family customs and traditions.
Celebrations and special occasions which occur annually.
Giving and receiving gifts.
Favourite stories and characters and the meanings they convey.
Attitudes towards each other.
The importance of ritual in everyday life.
Foods eaten on special occasions.
Groups to which they belong.

SYMBOLS
Signs and symbols in everyday life.
Light: divas; bonfires; sacred fire (arti).
Foods: offerings; milk; rice; coconuts; sweet meats; fruits; nuts.
Deities.
Colours.
Havan kund.
Prashad.
Rakhi.

Scheme of Work: Holi

- Indian foods, e.g. samosas, poppadoms, sweets (barfi), coconuts
- A tape of Indian music
- Images of Krishna

Setting the scene

Put the tablecloth in the centre of a fairly large space on the floor. Arrange the coloured tissue paper and the wood in the centre of the cloth to resemble a bonfire. Alternatively, place several Indian lamps in place of the wood. Place the artefacts, the garlands and the unlit divas and joss sticks on the cloth.

The activity

Play Indian music and invite children to sit around the outside edge of the circular cloth.

Give a brief explanation of the display and ask whether anyone can name any of the symbols on the cloth. What are they used for? Do any of the objects remind children of things which are used to celebrate special occasions in their own experience? Read a story associated with Holi (see below).

Invite one or two children to discover how the musical instruments are played. Ask what kinds of party foods children enjoy most when they celebrate at home. Name the Indian foods (if they are unfamiliar to the pupils). Talk about favourite foods. Pass the Indian food around and sample it.

Play Indian music and move around the circle in a clockwise direction. Some children might like to play finger cymbals or beat drums in time to the rhythm.

Lessen the volume of the music and ask everyone to stand still. Give each pupil a coloured streamer and explain that they are less messy than coloured water! Throw the streamers across the circle and wait for the excitement to settle.

Light the divas and the joss sticks, taking care there is no paper near them. Darken the room and spend a few moments enjoying the smell of the incense and the flickering flames of the divas.

Sensory learning experiences

Using the display described in the activities for Holi, which is also illustrated in the drawing, pupils might be encouraged to participate in learning experiences and to explore Hindu artefacts.

- Put a garland around your neck. See how you look in a mirror.
- Explore the musical instruments and discover the sounds which they make.
- Watch the dancing flames of the **divas** and enjoy the pungent smell of the incense sticks.
- Taste some Indian sweets.
- Enjoy the Indian music and join in some movement.
- Hold an image of **Krishna** on your lap. Trace the design of the image and its shape with your fingers.
- Notice the coolness of the brass from which the symbol Aum is made.
- Throw coloured streamers of confetti. Enjoy streamers winding around your body. Shake the confetti out of your hair.

COCONUT BARFI

Hindus often make sweets to eat and to give as gifts at festival times. Barfi is like fudge, and it is very easy to make.

255g sugar
115g desiccated coconut
8 tbsp water
60ml milk powder
1 tbsp. pistachio nuts
few drops food colouring

1. Grease a shallow baking tray.
2. Bring the water to the boil in a non-stick pan. Add the sugar and stir with a wooden spoon until a syrup forms. Bring to the boil and simmer for three minutes, stirring all the time.
3. Add the coconut, milk powder and a few drops of food colouring.
4. Mix thoroughly and place over a very gentle heat until the mixture is very thick.
5. Pour the mixture into the greased tin and scatter the nuts over the top.
6. Allow the Barfi to cool and cut into bite-size pieces.

A STORY FOR HOLI

Long ago in India there lived a holy man called Krishna who had special powers. When he was a child he was very mischievous and was always getting into trouble. One day he broke the milkmaids' pots. Another day he stole their clothes and hid them while they were swimming in the river Yamuna and hung them in the trees! Krishna's best friend was a girl called Radha who had beautiful dark hair. Often they would dance in the moonlight by the river and sometimes Krishna would play his flute. One evening when the moon was full, the milkmaids joined in the dancing and Radha sang while Krishna played beautiful music. Many other people joined in the fun.

Suddenly Krishna disappeared to the village and when he returned he had lots of pots full of coloured powder. Carefully he put the pots on the ground and then he called to Radha. She came running towards him and, just as she was next to him he threw a handful of red powder all over her. Radha was surprised and so was everyone else. They all stopped dancing and watched as Krishna threw yellow, blue and green powder over her. She picked up first one pot of powder and then all the colours in turn, throwing them over Krishna. Soon everyone was dong the same and the night was filled with the sound of laughter and beautiful colours.

From that time on every year in the springtime people in India celebrate Holi or the 'Festival of Colours' in memory of Krishna and Radha.

Holi

1. Divas in lanterns
2. Musical instruments
3. Aum Symbol
4. Coconut
5. Krishna
6. Incense sticks (joss sticks)

CHAPTER 7

Recording Pupil Achievement

The status of Religious Education as part of the Basic Curriculum but not the National Curriculum is important. Religious Education has equal standing in relation to the core and other foundation subjects within a school's curriculum, but it is not subject to nationally prescribed assessment.

Understanding religion demands that children learn 'about' and 'from' the beliefs, values and customs which underpin the faiths studied. Although the Dearing Review of the National Curriculum replaced Statements of Attainment with Level Descriptors, Statements of Achievement are used to support the schemes of work suggested in *RE for All*, since they have value as progressive statements of competence for pupils to develop.

The suggested framework of assessment uses the two Attainment Targets: **Knowledge and Understanding of Religion** and **Key Ideas and Questions Arising from Human Experience.** The Attainment Targets define the knowledge, skills and understanding which pupils of different abilities and maturities are expected to have gained by the end of each Key Stage. The first Attainment Target, Knowledge and Understanding of Religion, should include helping pupils to understand about beliefs, practices and lifestyles at each Key Stage and throughout each topic or theme.

Beliefs, for example:
  Belief in God
  Belonging to groups
  Stories about key figures and religious leaders
  Special books and sacred writings

Practices, for example:
  Special buildings and places of worship
  Features of worship and prayer
  Special times and rites of passage
  Festivals and celebrations
  Special journeys and pilgrimages

Lifestyles, for example:
  Rules
  Families
  Caring for the world around
  Commitment
  Religion and daily life

Both Attainment Targets are underpinned by the nine study units which have been interwoven throughout the Programmes of Study:

- Human Experience
- The World Around $\Big\}$ including lifestyles
- Special People/Key Figures and Leaders

RELIGIOUS EDUCATION

PUPIL RECORD

NAME David Richardo   Half Term Ending February 1996

Key Stage I

TOPIC OR THEME

Shabbat (Sabbath)

KNOWLEDGE AND UNDERSTANDING OF RELIGION

'Special Places' Understands there are special places where people worship
'Festivals and Celebrations' Helps to prepare and tastes foods associated with celebrations.

Learning Experiences

David helped to make challah bread.
David joined in a Shabbat meal and ate challah bread sprinkled with salt.

Statement of Achievement (including level)

David participated in the learning experiences and showed enjoyment when he was involved in kneading the dough for the challah loaf.

KEY IDEAS AND QUESTIONS ARISING FROM HUMAN

EXPERIENCE

David has been encouraged to think about special meals and occasions in his own home. He has helped to set the table for a special meal.

Learning Experiences

David has shared feelings about the importance of his family and friends.

Statement of Achievement (including level)

David was involved in choosing symbols which described the happy feelings he experiences when he is with his family. eg.

good feeling, great   hug   cheerful, happy,

51

- Special Books/Sacred Writings
- Special Buildings/Places of Worship
- Festivals and Celebrations
- Special Times/Rites of Passage
- Special Journeys/Pilgrimage
- Sign, Symbol and Language

The Level Descriptors have been selected in order that the achievements of *all* pupils may be recorded. They may be used as a guide to both the current performance of an individual pupil and as an indicator of how future progress may be made.

The Level Descriptors also indicate individual pupil reactions to the learning encounters provided through:

- **experiencing** the activity
- **awareness** of the activity
- **participation** in the activity
- **involvement** in the activity.

Teachers will need to show how pupils have demonstrated the Statements of Achievement. In many cases this will be supported by the Level Descriptors which describe the pupil involvement in the learning experiences provided. For example, the achievement of a pupil at the Foundation for Key Stage 1 within the study unit The World Around, might be recorded as: Responds to the natural world, with the comment, '... has shown an *awareness* of birds as they feed from the bird table, which has been demonstrated through her desire to sit near the window where she is able to watch'.

The use of Attainment Targets, Statements of Achievement and Level Descriptors will provide an important tool in enabling teachers to:

- **plan** future work, setting tasks and providing learning experiences appropriate to pupils' ability and development;
- **provide objectives** for pupils' learning ;
- **build** on the learning experiences provided and ensure continuity and progression to the next stage.

Foundation for Key Stage 1 Statements of Achievement

Human Experience
- Is beginning to develop an awareness of self
- Is beginning to develop an awareness of other people
- Is beginning to develop an awareness of belonging to a group
- Is beginning to develop self-control
- Is beginning to express emotions
- Hears a range of stories about human experience themes

The World Around
- Experiences the natural world
- Responds to the natural world
- Responds to different environments
- Experiences situations which may evoke a sense of awe and wonderment, e.g. raindrops on skin, snow flakes on skin; rolling in leaves; lying under a tree on a sunny day in dappled sunlight

Special People/Key Figures and Leaders
- Recognises special people in own family
- Recognises familiar people in school environment
- Recognises familiar people in the local community

Special Books/Sacred Writings
- Enjoys the tactile qualities of a book
- Shares a story book with an adult

- Listens to a favourite story about everyday experience
- Recognises favourite stories/books
- Begins to show an awareness of books which are special to other people

Special Buildings/Places of Worship
- Responds to the atmosphere in different environments within school
- Recognises familiar environments
- Experiences a variety of different religious buildings in the local community

Festivals and Celebrations
- Experiences sights, colours, smells, tastes, sounds associated with celebrations at home and at school
- Encounters a variety of religious celebrations

Special Times/Rites of Passage
- Shares photographs of special occasions in own life with an adult
- Responds to a milestone or special occasion celebrated in own life

Special Journeys/Pilgrimage
- Responds to own experience of journeys and travelling
- Participates in a special journey

Sign, Symbol and Language
- Experiences signs and symbols in everyday life
- Begins to show an awareness of symbols in everyday life
- Recognises some symbols associated with religious festivals and celebrations

End of Key Stage 1 Statements of Achievement
Human Experience
- Is developing an awareness of self in relation to others
- Is beginning to develop healthy self-esteem
- Is aware of own contribution as part of a group
- Demonstrates a degree of self-control
- Is beginning to demonstrate emotional responses to happenings in own life, e.g. happiness/sadness
- Demonstrates an awareness of other people's emotions
- Listens to a range of stories with human experience themes (e.g. families; friendship; loss and change) and is able to relate these to own experience.

The World Around
- Is able to identify different environments
- Expresses curiosity and interest at the world around
- Is beginning to be aware of how people care for living things and the local environment
- Has heard several creation stories

Special People/Key Figures and Leaders
- Meets members of faith communities
- Is aware that some people follow a religious way of life
- Identifies the key figures from a Bible story and a story from one other sacred book
- Is aware some people believe God to be important

Special Books/Sacred Writings
- Is aware that a story may be told for a specific purpose
- Is able to identify a story from the life or teaching of Jesus
- Is beginning to develop an awareness that holy books should be respected and handled carefully

- Can identify a Bible and knows the book comprises the Old and New Testaments

Special Buildings/Places of Worship
- Understands there are special places where people go to worship
- Has been introduced to some of the key points in a place of worship, e.g. altar, pulpit, font; quiblah, minbar; ark; shrine; langar
- Begins to demonstrate an awareness of the distinctive atmosphere of a religious place
- Begins to demonstrate respectful behaviour when visiting a place of worship
- Has encountered a variety of sensory experiences in places of worship, e.g. heard music; touched different materials from which buildings are constructed; smelt incense; watched candles/sacred lights burning; looked at and touched fabrics and embroidery

Festivals and Celebrations
- Is beginning to recognise there are times which have special significance for some people
- Helps to prepare and tastes a variety of foods associated with festivals from the religions studied
- Begins to recognise the importance of preparing for a festival or celebration
- Begins to show an awareness of the pattern of religious festivals for Christians and one other religion

Special Times/Rites of Passage
- Begins to show an awareness of special events and milestones within own life, e.g. staying away from home for the night; starting school; loosing a tooth
- Begins to show an awareness of special events within family life, e.g. birth/initiation ceremonies; coming of age; weddings
- Is helped to make a pictorial chart of special times in own life from birth to the present day

Special Journeys/Pilgrimage
- Experiences some different kinds of journeys and begins to recognise some of the reasons and motivations for these journeys
- Hears a first-hand account from someone who has been on a special journey or pilgrimage
- Brings to school a souvenir or memento of a special journey or a visit and explains to peer group the significance of the item

Sign, Symbol and Language
- Is beginning to develop a sensitivity towards the special meaning conveyed by some religious symbols, e.g. dress; food
- Is able to recognise symbols representative of the religious group to which they belong and/or the Christian tradition

End of Key Stage 2 Statements of Achievement

Human Experience
- Has increased knowledge of self
- Is able to reflect on own sense of uniqueness
- Is able to make choices
- Demonstrates an empathy towards key characters in stories with human experience themes
- Shows empathy towards the needs and feelings of people from a variety of faiths and cultures
- Shows sensitivity towards the lifestyles of other people within the school family and the local community

The World Around
- Demonstrates a sense of responsibility towards living things and the environment
- Participates in learning experiences which relate to environmental issues
- Begins to develop a concept of the interdependence of humankind and the created order

- Begins to recognise the commitment which religions have to the world in which we live
- Begins to appreciate the pain and beauty of the natural world
- Is beginning to reflect on existential questions of meaning and purpose

Special People/Key Figures and Leaders
- Is becoming aware of the importance of key figures and religious leaders, e.g. Jesus; Moses; Muhammad; Guru Nanak; Siddartha Gautama; through hearing stories and increasing knowledge of religious belief and practice
- Meets and interacts with leaders from the Christian community and two other religions

Special Books/Sacred Writings
- Can identify and name some holy books and recognises a story from the Christian Bible and one other story from another faith
- Shows awareness of the importance of religious books and sacred writings to some people
- Is able to identify and name holy books from the religions studied
- Is able to name some of the books of the Old and New Testaments in the Bible

Special Buildings/Places of Worship
- Has had opportunities to explore space within religious buildings
- Has visited a variety of local places of worship from the Christian tradition and other religions studied
- Demonstrates an ability for quiet reflection when visiting a place of worship
- Is able to identify some of the key points in a place of worship and to sign/explain why they are of significance to worshippers

Festivals and Celebrations
- Begins to explore the significance of shared meals and special foods, e.g. Pesach; the Eucharist
- Knows that Sunday is a special day for Christians and recognises the importance of a daily/weekly time of worship/reflection for some people
- Is able to retell through words/pictures/signs/symbols the Easter and Christmas stories as recorded in the Gospel narratives
- Is able to explain the significance of Easter for Christians

Special Times/Rites of Passage
- Has watched a video or experienced first-hand a baptism and wedding within the Christian tradition and a wedding and an initiation ceremony from one other religion studied
- Is able to talk about/sign or to explain in symbols the importance of family photographs, visual reminders and accounts as reminders of rites of passage
- Begins to understand the importance of ritual and symbol in rites of passage, e.g. water in baptism; the exchange of rings during the marriage service; sacred thread; sharing special food; flowers and memorials at funerals

Special Journeys/Pilgrimage
- Is able to identify several different reasons for making a journey
- Begins to understand the significance of artefacts and mementoes as reminders of a special journey
- Has visited a place of pilgrimage or a place which has special meaning for an individual or for a faith community, e.g. a cathedral; tomb or burial place
- Is helped to find in an atlas or on a globe significant places of pilgrimage from religions studied

Sign, Symbol and Language
- Has explored the symbol of the cross within Christianity and has encountered a variety of different crosses/crucifix within a Christian place of worship
- Begins to understand the importance of artefacts as a focus of attention or as an aid during prayer
- Is able to identify artefacts from own religious tradition (if appropriate) or the religions studied and is able to show they might be used by a member of the faith tradition
- Has experienced first-hand or through audio-visual aids a variety of forms of worship from the religions studied
- Begins to use appropriate language/signs/symbols for artefacts

CHAPTER 8

The Principal World Religions

Christianity

The roots of Christianity are in the Judaism of over two thousand years ago. Christianity appears in many different forms and about a third of the world's population are Christian. It is not easy to generalise about the belief and practices. However most Christians would agree with the following:

- There is one **God**, creator and sustainer of the world.
- God is personal in the sense that God can both speak to people and be addressed by them.
- **Jesus** was born as man in Bethlehem about 6 BCE. He was also God in human flesh. He died by crucifixion about 30 CE during the Roman occupation of Palestine. Three days afterwards he rose from the dead. Through this death and resurrection, those who believe in him are made righteous in God's sight and will, after a final judgement, reside in heaven.
- The power of God by which this salvation is accomplished is known as the **Holy Spirit**. The Holy Spirit guides and strengthens believers. God as Creator, as Redeemer in **Christ** and as Power in the Spirit continues a saving activity in the world. This belief is expressed in the doctrine of the **Trinity** which recognises that the mystery of God's oneness is more than can be expressed in 'one person'.
- The activity by which God redeems humankind is known as 'grace', a word which emphasises the sense of need for God's help. Grace is freely given by God.
- The sacred books (**Old Testament** and **New Testament**) are called the **Bible.** These are the authoritative scriptures for Christians although not all Christians consider them as direct messages from God.

Because of the changes and differences of the core beliefs of the Christian faith, there are now over 20,000 different denominations and traditions. In recent times, great emphasis has been placed on the ecumenical movement which seeks greater unity between the different groups. These include the Church of England, Roman Catholic, Protestant, Eastern Orthodox, Evangelical and Pentecostal Churches and Free Churches which include Afro Caribbean, Baptist, Methodist, Quaker, the Salvation Army, and United Reformed.

Church of England

The Church of England is also known as the **Anglican** Church.

Although the Church of England has its origins in England, today there are branches worldwide.

The Church of England retains close relationships with the Roman Catholic Church, particularly regarding belief and forms of worship.

Roman Catholic

Roman Catholics account for nearly a half of the world's Christians. Roman Catholics consider the **Pope** to be their spiritual leader, since he is believed to be the spiritual inheritor of Saint Peter, the leader of the apostles to whom Jesus entrusted his church.

CHRISTIANITY
Key Stage

KNOWLEDGE AND UNDERSTANDING OF CHRISTIANITY (including belief and practice)
The Church as a Christian community and a building.
Keeping Sunday as a holy day.
Christians call God 'Father' because they believe he loves them and cares for them.
Christians call God 'Creator' because they believe he made and cares for the world
Important ceremonies, e.g. baptisms, weddings
Types of writing in the Bible: stories; poems; sayings.
Special leaders: priests; ministers; elders.
People who have set a Christian example.
The two greatest commandments: "Love God' and 'Love your neighbour'.
The Bible as two testaments: Old and New.

LEARNING EXPERIENCES
Pupils could:
Consider the importance of rituals and ceremonies.
Encounter Easter and Christmas celebrations.
Look at and handle carefully some special books, e.g. family Bible.
Listen and respond to stories from the Christian Bible.
Talk about signs of new life in the world around them.
Visit a variety of Christian places of worship and learn the names of the key features, e.g. font, table, altar, pulpit.
Listen and respond to stories about the natural world and Creation.

Make a display of objects and symbols associated with Christian worship.
See how a Bible is read in church services.

KEY IDEAS AND QUESTIONS ARISING FROM HUMAN EXPERIENCE
Pupils should be encouraged to think about:
Books and other objects which are special to them or which have particular significance.
People they admire.
The importance of belonging to a group.
Why we believe some things and not others.
Special times of the year in their own lives.
Signs of belonging, e.g. uniforms, badges, symbols.
The importance of family life.

SYMBOLS
Cross.
Water.
Icon.
Bible.
Prayer-book; missal.
Font.
Pulpit.
Liturgical colours.

Scheme of Work: Christianity

MY CHURCH

I go to Church.

In Church we go to Sunday School. I draw pictures of my friends. We read a story about Jesus.

The Church is big and cold. I see some flowers. We sing. I like Lord of the dance.

We say prayers. I say Amen in a big voice. I talk to my friends at Church.

by Katie Carpenter

57

Eastern Orthodox

The word Orthodox means 'true' or 'right' worship. Therefore emphasis is placed on the value of traditional worship.

The Eastern Orthodox Church is made up of many national or regional churches, e.g. Serbian, Armenian, Russian and Greek. There is a self-governing system with each church having a **Patriarch,** or leader.

Protestant

Until the Reformation, the Roman Catholic and Orthodox Churches were the two main groupings of Christianity. However there was much unrest and 'protest' concerning the power of the Roman Catholic Church. Martin Luther, a German, and John Calvin, a Frenchman, disagreed with the authority of the Pope in Rome and Protestant Churches were formed. Today, in Germany and Scandinavia, the **Lutheran Church** is particulary strong.

Evangelical and Pentecostal

The Evangelical Church places particular emphasis on the **Gospel** and the scriptures as the sole authority in all matters of faith and conduct. Pentecostal Churches take their name from the Greek word 'pentecoste', the Jewish festival of Weeks or Shavuot, which comes seven weeks (fifty days) after Passover, when the followers of Jesus received the gift of the Holy Spirit, described in Acts 1-2. In modern form, Pentecostal Churches have their origin among the black and white people of the United States of America who were rejected by the established Churches in the early twentieth century. Worship places emphasis on singing, free prayer, and calling on the Holy Spirit to be received by all present.

Free Churches

Free Churches are also known as Non-conformist Churches. They have their origins in the English speaking churches of the seventeenth and eighteenth centuries. They are free from state control. The **Quaker Church** or the Religious Society of Friends was established through the work of George Fox in the seventeenth century.

The **Presbyterian Church** or the national church of Scotland is governed by 'elders' or 'presbyters'.

The **United Reformed Church** was formed by the union of English Congregationalists with the Presbyterian Church of England, whilst the **Baptist Church** grew out of the Anabaptist movement during the sixteenth-century Reformation, which in turn led to the formation of Protestant Churches.

The **Salvation Army** is also a Free Church, founded by William and Catherine Booth in the nineteenth century.

Worship

The most characteristic act of worship for Christians is a sacred meal in which bread and wine are shared together after they have been consecrated as a means of 'communion' with Christ and with one another. The sacred meal is known by various terms:

- Eucharist
- Holy Communion
- Lord's Supper
- Holy Liturgy
- Mass

Not all Christians use the sacrament, e.g. The Salvation Army and The Society of Friends or Quakers. The format of the service also varies widely throughout the world. Some Christians believe that, in the Mass, the bread and wine become the actual body and blood of Jesus. Other Christians regard the bread and wine as symbols of the body and blood in the service of Holy Communion.

Sacred writings

The first Christians were Jews and they looked to the Jewish scriptures to understand their experience of Jesus. Much of the Christian Bible therefore comprises Jewish scriptures in the Old Testament. The New Testament was added after the death of Jesus.

Readings from the Old Testament are used during Christian private and group worship. Perhaps the best known saying of Jesus used in worship is from the Sermon on the Mount found in Matthew's Gospel 6: 9-13. The Good News Bible reads:

Our Father in heaven:
May your holy name be honoured;
may your Kingdom come;
may your will be done on earth as
it is in heaven.
Give us today the food we need.
Forgive us the wrongs we have done,
as we forgive the wrongs that
others have done to us.
Do not bring us to hard testing,
but keep us safe from the Evil One.

Place of worship

The names of the buildings where Christian communities worship are most often called churches, although some denominations prefer to call them chapels. Many churches are built to resemble a cross with an **altar** or table at the east end where the sacred meal takes place in all but the churches of the Salvation Army and the Religious Society of Friends.

Churches (with the exception of Salvation Army and the Religious Society of Friends) also have a **font** or baptistery for infant or believer's baptism, a rite by which a person is admitted into the Christian Church.

Sunday is the holy day in commemoration of the day when Jesus rose from the dead; the day when God created the world and the day when the Holy Spirit came upon the apostles at Pentecost. Many Christians will however worship privately each day.

Festivals

Most Christian festivals commemorate important events in the life of Jesus. The Christian year follows both the lunar and a solar calendar and a cycle which relates to martyrs and saints. Christmas always take place on 25th December and follows the solar calendar. Therefore the festivals which are dependent on it occur at the same dates each year. Easter, however, is calculated from the cycle of the moon and therefore the date differs from year to year. The third cycle of festivals have specific dates set aside for them and are mostly celebrated by the Anglican, Roman Catholic and Orthodox Churches.

Advent

Advent marks the beginning of the Christian year on the fourth Sunday before Christmas in the Western calendar and forty days before Christmas in the Eastern Orthodox tradition. The word advent means 'coming' and it is a time when Christians prepare for Christmas. Some churches will have an **advent wreath** or crown with four candles, one of which is lit on each of the four Sundays.

Christmas

Christmas, or Christ's Mass, celebrates the birth of Jesus, although the exact date of his birth is not known. The festival was not celebrated until the fourth century CE. Traditionally churches have a crib or stable scene which depicts the Christmas story as recorded in the Gospels of Matthew and Luke. Many of the contemporary customs associated with Christmas have their origins in pre-Christian times.

Epiphany

The festival of Christmas ends with Epiphany, a word which means 'manifestation' or 'showing faith'. In the Western calendar the Magi or astrologers who brought gifts to the Christ Child in Matthew's Gospel are remembered. In the Eastern calendar, Epiphany celebrates the baptism of Jesus.

Lent

Lent is a period of penitence and preparation for the major Christian festival of Easter. It begins forty days before

┌───┐

CHRISTIAN HARVEST THANKSGIVING
Key Stage

KNOWLEDGE AND UNDERSTANDING OF CHRISTIANITY (including belief and practice)

Stories, songs, poems and sayings from the Bible which describe God as Creator and Sustainer.
The Bible as two Testaments: Old and New.
The Church as a Christian community.
Keeping Sunday as a holy day.
The importance of special times to the Christian community.
Christian values: self-sacrifice, commitment, love.

LEARNING EXPERIENCES

Pupils could:
Encounter a celebration of Harvest Thanksgiving.
Share feelings about gratitude and thankfulness.
Hear and respond to readings from the Bible about God as Creator and Provider.
Hear some of the prayers used during a Harvest Thanksgiving and talk about the feelings and beliefs they express.
Listen and respond to stories about the natural world and Creation.
Visit a church decorated for Harvest and respond to the displays.
Distinguish between what is made by people and what belongs to the natural world.
Experience and talk about the care of living things.
Share feelings associated with awe and wonderment.
Find out how Harvest is celebrated by Christians throughout the world.

KEY IDEAS AND QUESTIONS ARISING FROM HUMAN EXPERIENCE

Pupils should be encouraged to think about:
The importance of belonging to a group.
The dependence/interdependence of the world/humankind.
How some of the parables of Jesus relate to their own lives.
Special times of the year in their own lives.
What people need for their survival.
Saying 'please' and 'thank you'.
People who care for them.
Giving and receiving gifts.

SYMBOLS

Bread.
Wine.
Harvest gifts: fruits of the earth/sea/industry/humankind.

Scheme of Work: Christian Harvest Thanksgiving

Easter and the final week before Easter or **Holy Week** is a time when the Passion narratives from the Gospels are read. Holy Week commences with **Palm Sunday** when Jesus's triumphant entry into Jerusalem is remembered, and in some churches palm crosses may be distributed to the congregation and a Passion Narrative may be read. On the Thursday of Holy Week or **Maundy Thursday** some priests wash the feet of members of their congregation as a re-enactment of Jesus's action to the apostles at the Last Supper.

Good Friday commemorates the death of Jesus. In some communities three-hour services are held from noon until three o'clock in the afternoon, which is held to be the time when Jesus was being crucified on the cross.

Easter Sunday

Easter is the major festival of the Christian Church which celebrates the resurrection of Jesus. In some churches a vigil is kept for the whole of the Saturday night before. In Orthodox Churches, Easter is welcomed at midnight on **Holy Saturday** and the congregation may receive candles as a symbol of light triumphing over darkness, or resurrection over death. The early Christians often baptised new members into the church on Easter Day and this tradition has continued in some twentieth-century communities.

Ascension Day

Ascension Day is forty days after Easter when Jesus's ascension to heaven is celebrated (Luke 24: 50-51; Acts: 1 1-11). Ascension Day always falls on a Thursday. Although there are no widespread traditions associated with the festival, some churches will celebrate a special Eucharist and for many Christians it is a holiday.

Pentecost

The name Pentecost is taken from the Greek word 'pentecoste' meaning fiftieth day. The festival is celebrated on the seventh Sunday after Easter and it completes the Easter cycle. Originally the celebration was a Jewish one – the day after the seventh sabbath after Passover. The Christian church gave the festival another meaning,

Christian Harvest Thanksgiving

1. Pumpkin
2. Fruits of the earth
3. Breads
4. Corn

celebrating the day as the time when the gift of the Holy Spirit was given to the apostles (Acts: 2 1-11). The Anglo Saxon name for Pentecost is 'White Sunday' (Whitsunday) since, like Easter, the day became a popular time for baptism when white garments would have been worn.

Although Christian communities remember the festival and the readings for the day will include the account from the Book of Acts, some of the traditions associated with the day may have pre-Christian origins, e.g. the 'Whit Walk' and 'Well-dressing' which still take place in the north of England.

Glossary

Advent	Coming. The period beginning on the fourth Sunday before Christmas (40 days before Christmas in the Eastern Orthodox tradition). A time of spiritual preparation for Christmas.
Altar	Table used for Eucharist, Mass, Lord's Supper. Some denominations refer to it as Holy Table or Communion Table.
Anglican	Churches in full communion with the See of Canterbury. Their origins and traditions are linked to the Church of England, and are part of the Anglican Communion.
Apostle	One who was sent out by Jesus Christ to preach the Gospel.
Ascension Day	The event, 40 days after the Resurrection, when Jesus 'ascended into heaven' (see Luke 24 and Acts 1).
Baptism	Rite of initiation involving immersion in, or pouring of, water.
Baptist	(i) A member of the Baptist Church, which grew out of the Anabaptist movement during the Reformation. (ii) A Christian who practises Believer's Baptism.
Baptistery (or Baptistry)	(i) Building or pool used for baptism, particularly by immersion. (ii) Part of a church, where baptism takes place.
Christ (Messiah)	The anointed one. Messiah is used in the Jewish tradition to refer to the expected leader sent by God, who will bring salvation to God's people. Jesus's followers applied this title to him, and its Greek equivalent, Christ, is the source of the words Christian and Christianity.
Christmas	Festival commemorating the birth of Jesus Christ (25 December, in most Churches).
Church	(i) The whole community of Christians. (ii) The building in which Christians worship. (iii) A particular denomination.
Church of England	Also known as the Anglican Church.
Congregationalist	Member of a Christian body which believes that each local church is independent and self-governing under the authority of Christ.
Easter	Central Christian festival which celebrates the resurrection of Jesus Christ from the dead.
Eastern Orthodox	Consists of national churches (mainly Greek and Slav), including the ancient Patriarchates.
Epiphany	The sixth of January in the Western calendar which marks the end of Christmas and the arrival of the 'Magi' who brought gifts to the Christ Child. In the Eastern calendar, Epiphany marks Jesus's baptism.
Eucharist	Thanksgiving. A service celebrating the sacrificial death and resurrection of Jesus Christ, using elements of bread and wine (see Holy Communion).
Evangelical	Group, or church, placing particular emphasis on the Gospel and the scriptures as the sole authority in all matters of faith and conduct.
Font	Receptacle to hold water used in baptism.
Free Churches	Non-conformist denominations, free from state control.
Good Friday	The Friday in Holy Week. Commemorates the day Jesus died on the cross.
Gospel	(i) Good news (of salvation in Jesus Christ). (ii) An account of Jesus's life and work.
Holy Communion	Central liturgical service observed by most Churches (see Eucharist, Mass, Lord's Supper, Liturgy). Recalls the last meal of Jesus, and celebrates his sacrificial and saving death.
Holy Liturgy	A service of worship in the Eastern Orthodox Church which includes the Eucharist.
Holy Spirit	The third person of the Holy Trinity. Active as divine presence and power in the world, and in dwelling in believers to make them like Christ and empower them to do God's will.

Holy Week	The week before Easter, when Christians recall the last week of Jesus's life on Earth.
Icon	Painting or mosaic of Jesus Christ, the Virgin Mary, a saint, or a Church feast. Used as an aid to devotion, usually in the Orthodox tradition.
Jesus Christ	The central figure of Christian history and devotion. The second person of the Trinity.
Lectern	Stand supporting the Bible, often in the shape of an eagle.
Lent	Penitential season. The 40 days leading up to Easter.
Lord's Supper	Alternative term for Eucharist in some Churches (predominantly Non-conformist).
Lutheran	A major Protestant Church that received its name from the sixteenth-century German reformer, Martin Luther.
Mass	Term for the Eucharist, used by the Roman Catholic and other Churches.
Maundy Thursday	The Thursday in Holy Week. Commemorates the Last Supper.
Methodist	A Christian who belongs to the Methodist Church which came into existence through the work of John Wesley in the eighteenth century.
Missal	Book containing words and ceremonial directions for saying Mass.
New Testament	Collection of 27 books forming the second section of the Canon of Christian Scriptures.
Non-conformist	Protestant Christian bodies which became separated from the established Church of England in the seventeenth century.
Old Testament	The part of the Canon of Christian Scriptures which the Church shares with Judaism, comprising 39 books and, in the case of certain denominations, some books of the Apocrypha.
Palm Sunday	The Sunday before Easter, commemorating the entry of Jesus into Jerusalem when he was acknowledged by crowds waving palm branches.
Passion	The sufferings of Jesus Christ, especially in the time leading up to his crucifixion.
Patriarch	Title for principal Eastern Orthodox bishops. Also used for early Israelite leaders such as Abraham, Isaac, Jacob.
Pentecost (Whitsun)	The Greek name for the Jewish Festival of Weeks, or Shavuot, which comes seven weeks ('fifty days') after Passover. On the day of this feast, the followers of Jesus received the gift of the Holy Spirit.
Pentecostal	A Church that emphasises certain gifts which were granted to the first believers on the Day of Pentecost (such as the power to heal the sick and speak in tongues).
Pope	The Bishop of Rome, head of the Roman Catholic Church.
Presbyterian	A member of a Church that is governed by elders or 'presbyters'; the national Church of Scotland.
Protestant	That part of the Church which became distinct from the Roman Catholic and Orthodox Churches when their members professed (or 'protested' – hence Protestant) the centrality of the Bible and other beliefs. Members affirm that the Bible, under the guidance of the Holy Spirit, is the ultimate authority for Christian teaching.
Pulpit	An elevated platform from which sermons are preached.
Quaker	A member of the Religious Society of Friends, established through the work of George Fox in the seventeenth century.
Roman Catholic	That part of the Church owing loyalty to the Bishop of Rome, as distinct from Orthodox and Protestant Churches.
Salvation Army	A Free Church founded by William and Catherine Booth in the nineteenth century.
Trinity	Three persons in one God; doctrine of the threefold nature of God – Father, Son and Holy Spirit.
United Reformed Church	A Church formed by the union of English Congregationalists and subsequently the Reformed Association of the Churches of Christ.
Whit Sunday	The Anglo Saxon name for the festival of Pentecost or 'White Sunday' celebrated on the seventh Sunday after Easter.

Judaism

The Jewish people believe in one God who is Creator and Sovereign Lord. Jewish beliefs and practice are based on the first five books of the Bible, known as the Torah (Law) and the views of rabbis down the centuries. From the earliest times of Israel's faith an oral tradition grew up. This is known as the Oral Torah. In about 200 CE the Oral Torah was written down and it became known as the Mishnah. Commentaries on the Mishnah were written called Gemara and the two were combined together about 500 CE and became known as the Talmud.

There are two main groups of Jews today; the **Sephardim** and the **Ashkenazim**. The Jewish people believe in one God who is Creator and Sovereign Lord. The Sephardim Jews are descended from Jews in Spain and Portugal and they form the smaller group in Great Britain. Ashkenazim Jews' cultural origins are from Germany and Eastern Europe and their culture is associated with the **Yiddish** language, a mixture of German and Hebrew. There are four main types of Judaism practised today: Ultra-Orthodox Judaism; Orthodox Judaism; Reform Judaism; Liberal and Progressive Judaism.

Ultra-Orthodox

This group represents a strict adherence to the **Commandments** given in the Torah, applying them to all aspects of daily life. The largest community lives in the Mea Sherim area of Jerusalem. In Great Britain Ultra-Orthodox Jews are to be found among other areas in the Stamford Hill area of London, Gateshead and Manchester. Many adherents will wear conservative style dress and men often have their hair in side locks and have a beard. Women wear long dresses with long sleeves and many will keep their head covered. Many Ultra-Orthodox Jews come from large families. They are often typified in Britain by the Lubavitch Jews.

Orthodox

Towards the end of the nineteenth century large numbers of Jews left Eastern Europe and with this uprooting came a more open attitude to the culture of the modern West. Orthodox Jews centre their lives on the teaching (mitzvah) of the Torah but they are often prepared to adapt their religious practice, in a limited way, to the demands of the culture in which they live, so long as the two do not conflict.

Religious laws concerning the home, food and the Sabbath are carefully observed, together with attendance at the synagogue and the observance of religious festivals. Children of Orthodox Jews will attend Jewish schools wherever possible.

In the synagogue women sit separately from the men and they do not read from the Torah during services.

Reform Judaism

The Reform movement began in Germany at the beginning of the eighteenth century. Men and women worship together in Reform Synagogues. Festivals will be observed at home and in the synagogue, together with dietary laws.

Liberal and Progressive Judaism

Liberal Judaism resulted from Reformed Judaism in the nineteenth century. Although the teachings of the Torah are largely observed, adherence to Jewish law is not always strict. Men and women worship together (using their national language) and in more recent times there have been female rabbis.

Festivals are observed but some more strictly than others. For example some Liberal Jews will not attend synagogue each Saturday but they will celebrate holy days.

The **Sabbath** (or Shabbat) is kept as a weekly celebration which lasts for 25 hours starting at sunset on Friday evening. It is a day of prayer, study and relaxation celebrated at home and in the synagogue.

The **Shema** is often recited twice daily by Jews. It is an affirmation of the oneness of God, the completeness with which he must be served and the commandments.

Hear, O Israel: The Lord is our God, The Lord, the One and Only.
You shall love the Lord, your God, with all your heart, with all your soul and with all your resources. Let these matters that I command you today be upon your heart. Teach them thoroughly to your children, and speak of them while you sit in your home, while you walk on the way, when you retire and when you arise. Bind them as a sign upon your arm and let them be signs between your eyes. And write them on the doorposts of your house and upon your gates. (Deuteronomy 6:5-9)

Festivals

Rosh Hashanah (New Year)

This occurs during September-October in the Western calendar. It is also known as 'The Day of Judgement'. In the synagogue a special feature of the festival is the blowing of the **shofar** or ram's horn which commemorates the near sacrifice of Abraham's son. In the afternoon in some traditions Jews may walk to a river and empty their pockets to symbolise a new start. Traditionally apples are eaten dipped in honey and bread may be made in the shape of a crown or a ladder.

Yom Kippur (Day of Atonement)

Yom Kippur is observed in September or October in the Western calendar, ten days after Rosh Hashanah. It is a solemn day of fasting when Jews confess their sins and ask God for forgiveness. There are four reasons why fasting takes place:

- to show sincerity to God
- to encourage self-discipline
- to concentrate the spirit
- to become more aware of other people.

In the synagogue a passage is often read from Leviticus 16 about the scapegoat sent into the wilderness to take away guilt:

> The community of Israel shall give Aaron two male goats for a sin-offering and a ram for a burnt-offering...The goat chosen for Azazel shall be presented alive to the Lord and sent off into the desert in order to take away the sins of the people.

(NB The meaning of Azazel is unknown but it may refer to a desert demon.)

Sukkot

Sukkot is also known as 'Tabernacles'. It is celebrated at the time of the Jewish harvest in September-October of the Western calendar. Families build a **sukkah** or temporary hut and live in it for a week. Four plants play a particular role at Sukkot. Their shapes symbolise different parts of the human body which can be used to worship God. The **lulav** or date palm represents the back and is a symbol of an upright life; **myrtle** symbolise the eyes and clear vision and hope; **willow** represents the mouth and honesty and the **etrog** or citron the heart and deep feelings and sincere relationships.

Simchat Torah

Simchat Torah is also known as 'Rejoicing of the Law'. The festival occurs at the end of Sukkot and symbolises the beginning of the reading from the Torah for the following year.

In the synagogue the Torah scrolls are often processed seven times. Children may wave flags, sometimes with an apple stuck on the top.

Hanukkah

Hanukkah is also known as the 'Festival of Dedication' or the 'Festival of Lights'. It occurs during December in the Western calendar and remembers how in the second century BCE, when Judah was occupied by Syrian Greeks, a fierce battle took place and the Jews won against all the odds. They were able to restore the Temple which their enemies had destroyed. However there was very little oil to fuel the perpetual light, but a miracle was worked and it remained alight for eight days until the fresh supply arrived. Hanukkah is therefore celebrated for eight days in mid-winter.

Purim

Purim or the festival of 'Lots' is celebrated in February or March in the Western calendar. It commemorates the saving of the Persian Jews by the intervention of Queen Esther 2,300 years ago. In synagogues on Purim, the book of Esther is read aloud and it is a time for fun. Whenever the name of Haman, who sought to persecute the Jews, is mentioned people boo and stamp their feet, blow a trumpet or wave a **gregger** (like a football rattle). People may also wear fancy dress. The following narrative is often read from The Prayer Book:

> We thank you for the wonders, for the heroic acts, for the victories, for the marvellous and consoling deeds which you performed to our fathers in those days at this season. In the days of Mordechai and Ester, in Shushan the capital, when the wicked Haman rose up against them, he sought to destroy, kill and exterminate all Jews, both young and old, little children and women, on one day, and plunder their possessions...then you, in your great mercy, upset his plan and overthrew his design, and made his acts recoil upon his own head. And you performed a wonder and a marvel for them, therefore we thank your great name.

Pesach

The week long festival of Pesach occurs during March or April in the Western calendar. It commemorates the exodus of the Hebrew people out of slavery in Egypt. The celebration is of central importance to Jewish belief and practice. The foundation of the story is to be found in Exodus 12. The highlight of Pesach is the Passover or **Seder** meal where Jews remember their slavery in the past and look forward to freedom for all people in the future.

Shavuot (Feast of Weeks)

Shavuot, like Pesach and Sukkot, commemorates the time when the Jews wandered in the wilderness after leaving slavery. It is celebrated seven weeks and a day after Pesach at the summer harvest. Shavuot remembers the giving of the **Torah** from God to Moses on Mount Sinai and all the celebrations focus on the Torah. Many Jews will spend the entire night before Shavuot studying parts of the Torah. Synagogues are decorated with flowers and the traditional foods are based on milk, e.g. pancakes filled with cream cheese (blintzes) and cheesecake.

Place of Worship

Jews gather for communal worship in a **synagogue,** a name which means 'gathering place'. The focal point of the synagogue is the **Ark,** a special cupboard where the Torah scrolls are kept. Many Jewish men will cover their heads with a **kippah** and some will wear a prayer shawl or **tallit.** Orthodox Jewish men will also wear **tephillin,** two small boxes containing the words of the Shema – one fastened to the arm and the other to the forehead.

Dietary rules

Many Jews eat only **kosher** or 'proper' or 'fit' food. Some foods such as fish which do not have fins and scales and shellfish are forbidden. Eating pork is not allowed or animals which do not have cloven hooves and chew the cud. All meat which is allowed must be ritually slaughtered in a painless and humane way. The mixing of meat and milk is also forbidden. Therefore cooking utensils for meat and milk are kept separately and the eating of these two foods at the same meal is not permitted. The laws relating to diet are found in Leviticus 14: 3-21.

Judaism
Key Stage

KNOWLEDGE AND UNDERSTANDING OF JUDAISM (including belief and practice)

Israel as a special place for Jewish families.
Family and community life.
Responsibility to God: the Shema; mezuzah; tallit; kippah; the Ten Commandments.
Special places: the Synagogue, Jerusalem.
Special times: Shabbat and the Friday night meal; Pesach; Bar Mitzvah; Bat Mitzvah.

LEARNING EXPERIENCES

Pupils could:
Find out the names of the books of the Torah.
Talk about characters in stories, and reflect on what sort of example they give other people to follow.
Share experiences of the celebrations they enjoy.
Share feelings about the importance of family and friends.
Listen to passages from the Torah.
Visit a synagogue.
Find Israel on a globe or in an atlas.
Examine a mezuzah and its contents, and talk about why it is important.
Look at and talk about some of the symbols associated with Jewish dress, e.g. tallit, kippah, tefillin.
Share any prayers which are special to them with the rest of the class.

KEY IDEAS AND QUESTIONS ARISING FROM HUMAN EXPERIENCE

Pupils should be encouraged to think about:
What is important and special to them.
Homes which they know.
Special times of the year in their own lives.
Signs of belonging, e.g. uniforms, badges, symbols.
Books which are special to them.
Family members who live at home and those who live somewhere else.
Rules and why they are important.

SYMBOLS

Magen-David.
Menorah.
Kippah.
Mezuzah.
Tefillin.
Bible.
Candles.
Sefer Torah.

Scheme of Work: Judaism

Glossary

Many of the terms used are Hebrew in origin. There are often acceptable differences in the ways in which words are spelt.

Ark	A special cupboard in the synagogue where the Torah scrolls are kept.
Bar Mitzvah	Son of Commandment. A boy's coming of age at 13 years old, usually marked by a synagogue ceremony and family celebration.
Bat Mitzvah	Daughter of Commandment. As above, but for girls from 12 years old. May be marked differently between communities.
Bimah	Dais. Raised platform primarily for reading the Torah in the synagogue.
Challah	Enriched bread used particularly on Shabbat and during festivals.
Gemara	Commentary on the Mishnah included in the Talmud.
Gregger	A rattle used in the synagogue when the name of wicked Haman is mentioned at Purim.
Hagadah	Telling. A book used at Seder.
Hanukkah	Dedication. An eight-day festival of lights to celebrate the re-dedication of the temple following the Maccabean victory over the Greeks.
Havdalah	Distinction. Ceremony marking the conclusion of Shabbat.
Kippah	Head covering worn during prayers, Torah study, etc. Some followers wear it constantly.
Magen-David	Shield of David; popularly called Star of David.
Menorah	Seven-branched candelabrum which was lit daily in the Temple.
Mezuzah	A scroll placed on doorposts of Jewish homes, containing a section from the Torah and often enclosed in a decorative case.
Mishnah	The written down Oral Torah.
Mitzvah	Commandment. The Torah contains 613 Mitzvot. Commonly used to describe good deeds.
Ner Tamid	Eternal light. The perpetual light above the Aron Hakodesh.
Pesach	Festival commemorating the Exodus from Egypt. One of the three biblical pilgrim festivals. Pesach is celebrated in the spring.
Purim	Festival commemorating the rescue of Persian Jews as told in the book of Esther.
Seder	Order. A home-based ceremonial meal during Pesach, at which the Exodus from Egypt is recounted using the Hagadah.
Shabbat	Day of spiritual renewal and rest commencing at sunset on Friday, terminating at nightfall on Saturday.
Shavuot	Weeks. One of three pilgrim festivals. Shavuot is celebrated in the summer, seven weeks after Pesach.
Shema	Major Jewish prayer affirming belief in one God. The Shema is found in the Torah.
Simchat Torah	Rejoicing of the law. Festival celebrating the completion and recommencement of the cycle of the weekly Torah reading.
Sukkah	Tabernacle; booth. A temporary dwelling used during Sukkot.
Sukkot	One of three biblical pilgrim festivals, Sukkot is celebrated in the autumn.
Synagogue	Building for Jewish public prayer, study and assembly.
Tallit	Prayer shawl. Four-cornered garment with fringes.
Talmud	Mishnah and Gemara, collected together.
Tefillin / tephillin / phylacteries	Small leather boxes containing passages from the Torah, strapped on the forehead and arm for morning prayers on weekdays.
Torah	Law; teaching. The Five Books of Moses.
Yiddish	Language used predominantly by Ashkenazim.
Yom Kippur	Day of Atonement. Fast day occurring on the tenth day after Rosh Hashanah; a solemn day of Tefillah and Teshuva.

Islam

Islam is a way of life based on faith and action which is summed up in the Five Pillars of faith. There are about one billion Muslims worldwide. The fundamental doctrine of Islam is that there is one God, who is creator of the universe. He is omnipotent and omniscient, and all humankind will be accountable to Him alone on the Day of Judgement. Muslims believe that Islam teaches a true and successful way of life for the whole of humankind.

Prophet Muhammad was born in Makkah in 570 CE. His parents died when he was very young and, for most of his childhood, he was brought up by his uncle, Abu Talib. He was married in his mid-twenties to a wealthy widow called Khadijah and, according to Muslim tradition, he became disillusioned with life and began to spend time alone in prayer and meditation. It was in a cave in Mount Hira that Muhammad began to receive revelations from Allah through the angel **Jibril** (Gabriel). Muhammad could neither read nor write but he learned the revelations by heart and dictated them to scribes. The completed revelations are recorded in the Qur'an and give detailed guidance on moral and ethical codes of behaviour.

In about 622 CE Muhammad was commanded by Allah to leave Makkah and he went to Yathrib where the entire community was converted to Islam and the town became known as **Madinatu'n-Nabi** or the 'City of the Prophet'. In 630 CE Muhammad was acknowledged by the people of Makkah as The Prophet of God and the first **mosque** was built there on his arrival.

Muhammad died in 632 CE. After his death he was succeeded by Abu Bakr as the first Caliph. After the death of the third Caliph Muslims differ about the succession. Two main groups developed. The **Sunnis** or 'followers of the Tradition' (sunnah) formed the majority. The **Shi'ites** took a different view, believing the only legitimate leaders of the community were Muhammad's descendants through his daughter Fatima and son-in-law Ali. Later different schools of thought emerged who formulated their own doctrines and interpretations of the Qur'an and the Tradition.

Although Islam is based on the revelations revealed to the Prophet, the religion is considered by Muslims to have originated with the creation of mankind and to have been revealed by God to all the prophets from Adam to Muhammad, who was the last. Indeed the Qur'an refers to this in Surah 3:83:

In the name of God, the most Beneficent, the Most Merciful
Say: 'We believe in God and the revelation given to us;
We believe in the revelations given to Abraham,
Ishmael, Isaac, Jacob and the tribes,
And to Moses and to Jesus and the other prophets.
We make no distinction between them
And we bow to God.'

The majority of Muslims today are Sunnis who strive to live their lives according to four schools of thought based directly on the Qur'an. **Shi'ah Islam** is the national religion of Iran and there are large numbers of followers in most of the Gulf States, India, Pakistan, Syria and Iraq.

Sacred writings

The sacred writings of Islam are contained in the Qur'an, which is always read in Arabic. The teachings of the Prophet were explained by him during his lifetime. They were recorded by his household and followers and are called the **Hadith.** Together with the record of model practices and traditions of the Prophet (**Sirah**), they contribute to the **Sunnah.**

The opening chapter or **Surah** of the Qur'an reads:

In the name of Allah The Compassionate The Merciful
Praise be to God, Lord of the Universe,
The Merciful, the Mercy-Giving!
Ruler of the Day for Repayment!
You do we worship and from You do we seek help.
Guide us along the Straight Road,
the Road of those whom You have favoured,
With whom you are not angry,
nor who are lost.

Basic Beliefs

There are seven basic beliefs in Islam. These are:

* Belief in One God
* Belief in the Angels of Allah

- Belief in the Books of Allah
- Belief in the Messengers of Allah
- Belief in the Day of Judgement
- Belief in the Supremacy of Divine Will
- Belief in Life after Death

The Five Pillars of Islam

Islam is sometimes compared to a house with firm foundations and a supportive structure: the 'Five Pillars' make specific requirements on all adherents to the faith:

Shahadah

Shahadah is the declaration of faith in Allah as the one and only God and Muhammad as the messenger of Allah. The basis of the declaration is the acceptance in public of belief in God and that Muhammad is his messenger.

Salah

Muslims should offer prayers five times each day. Each prayer consists of a number of **rak'ahs** or forms of words and order of movements. The times for prayer are: early morning after dawn; midday; afternoon; after sunset and at night. Physical and mental preparation is required for prayer. **Wudu,** which means 'washing certain parts of the body before prayer', is necessary. If water is not available, symbolic cleansing is done by striking clean sand or dust with both hands and wiping the face and back of the hands only.

There is a fixed order for wudu: hands up to the wrists (3 times); mouth rinsed (3 times); nostrils washed and nose blown (3 times); face washed (3 times); right hand and arm up to the elbow (3 times); left hand and arm up to the elbow (3 times); wet hands run over head and neck (once); ears washed (once); right foot washed as far as the ankle (3 times); left foot washed as far as the ankle (3 times).

Sawm

Observance of the monthly fast in the ninth month of the lunar year is the fourth pillar or duty of Islam. This involves total abstinence from food and drink, smoking and conjugal relations from just before dawn to sunset for the entire month. During the month of Ramadan Muslims are expected to purify their fasting by giving the price of one meal for each member of the family to needy persons.

Zakah

Giving and welfare is a central tenet of Islam. Zakah is two and a half percent of a person's saving given annually for the poor.

Hajj

For most Muslims Hajj is the most demanding and challenging of the five pillars. Hajj is an Arabic word meaning 'to set out with a definite purpose' and it refers to the duty of all Muslims to visit Makkah at least once during their life time. Many pilgrims travel by air before the 8th of the last month of the Islamic calendar to Jeddah and then follow the route which was taken by the Prophet to Makkah. Pilgrim dress or **ihram** is worn for the final part of the journey. Pilgrims circle the **Ka'bah** seven times, kissing, touching or raising their arms towards the Black Stone as they pray. Later they travel the road between the two hills associated with Hajar and Ishmael (at **Safa** and **Marwah**) seven times. After sunrise on the ninth day of the month they walk or ride to Mount **Arafat,** offer prayer to Allah and at sunset they continue to travel to **Muzdalifah** to say evening prayers. On the tenth day a journey is made to **Mina** where, during the following three days, stones are thrown at three pillars which represent the devil which tempted Ishmael. An animal is sacrificed and, finally, the Ka'bah is circled once again, and pilgrim clothes are removed and washed ready to be kept as a shroud for death. Having completed the journey pilgrims may prefix their name with **hajji** (male) or **hajjah** (female).

Festivals

The Muslim calendar is based on the **hijrah** or emigration of the Prophet Muhammad from Makkah to Medina in the year 622 CE. This year was adopted as the first year in the Muslim era. The calendar is a lunar one, having twelve months which are counted from one new moon to the next. Each month has twenty-nine or thirty days. Because the Muslim year is ten or eleven days shorter than the solar year, the months rotate around the seasons.

The festivals of Islam are called **Id**, an Arabic word which may be translated as 'recurring happiness'.

The sixth day of the week marks a time when most faithful Muslims meet together to worship. The importance of Friday communal worship or **Salat-ul-Jumu'ah** is referred to in the Qur'an 62:9:

> In the name of God, the Most Beneficent, the Most Merciful
> O Believers, when you are called to prayer on Friday
> Hasten earnestly to the remembrance of God
> And cease your trading.
> That is best for you.
> Then, when the prayer is finished,
> Disperse and go in search of God's bounty.
> Praise God always, so that you may prosper.

After the call to prayer the **Imam** gives a sermon to the congregation in the language of the community, save for the opening and closing remarks which are in Arabic. The Imam reminds the people of their duties towards God and towards other people. He may also speak on topics such as current affairs or events within the community, offering guidance and advice.

Ramadan

Observance of the monthly fast in the ninth month of the lunar year is the fourth pillar or duty of Islam. This involves total abstinence from food, drink, smoking and conjugal relations from just before dawn to sunset for the entire month. Persons who are very old, sick, young children and those who are travelling may be exempted. Only the sick are required to compensate by fasting for an equal number of days at a later time when they are healthy.

During the month of Ramadan, Muslims are also expected to give welfare dues or **zakah-ul-fitr**. This is equivalent to the price of one meal for each member of the family.

There are regional and cultural differences in the way in which Ramadan is observed, but striving to fulfil the commands of Allah through self-discipline, piety and collective worship are held to be of great importance. Each evening at sunset the fast is broken at the mosque by drinking water and eating dates, evening prayers are said and then families return home to share a meal.

Festival of Breaking the Fast

The fast of Ramadan ends with the three day festival of 'Breaking the Fast', on the first day of the following month. It is known as **Id-ul-Fitr** and is a time for rejoicing in God's favour. The Prophet is recorded as saying in the Hadith:

> When Id-ul-Fitr arrives, the angels stand at the doorways and call upon Muslims: O company of Muslims, go to the generous God, who gave you the good things and grants the great reward. For God ordered you to pray during the night, so you prayed, ordered you to fast during the day, so you fasted and obeyed your Lord, so now take your reward.

Id-ul-Fitr is also a festival of alms-giving when those Muslims who have not paid zakah during Ramadan are able to do so before Id prayer.

The festival begins at the mosque about an hour after sunset and the night of Id is traditionally spent in meditation and prayer. Id-ul-Fitr is traditionally a time for giving gifts and children are often given new clothes and presents.

Id-ul-Adha

Id-ul-Adha is also called the 'Festival of Sacrifice', or the 'Greater Festival', since it lasts for four days, a day longer than the other major festivals of Islam. It commemorates the willingness of Ibrahim to sacrifice his son. The festival is the day of sacrifice for Muslims on pilgrimage to Makkah but it is also celebrated throughout the Muslim world. Every Muslim who can afford to do so sacrifices an animal and shares the meat among family members, giving a major proportion to people who are poor and needy. The sacrifice is symbolic of obedience to God and readiness to sacrifice desires and worldly possessions for God's sake.

The Prophet's farewell sermon is also remembered at the time of the festival. The sermon sums up the principles of Islam and ends with an exhortation to Muslims to follow the teachings of the Qur'an and the Tradition of the Prophet.

The Prophet's Birthday

The festival is traditionally celebrated on the twelfth day of the third month. The celebration, which is also known

70

as **Mawlid an Nabi,** was introduced during the tenth century CE. There is great diversity in the way in which the festival is celebrated and some communities will not mark the day at all. Indeed, the day is a public holiday in only very few places.

On the festival there may be marches, and people often wear new clothes and prepare special food. In Malaya people gather in public places to listen to readings from the Qur'an and join in religious chants. In India, Pakistan and Bangladesh, songs are sung in honour of the Prophet and people attend lectures about the Prophet's life.

Place of worship

The building used for worship is known as a **masjid** or **mosque.** The word masjid may be translated as 'a place of prostration'. The prayer hall is of central importance to the building. There may also be places set aside as classrooms, administrative areas, storerooms, kitchens, mortuary, etc. The prayer hall is spacious and carpeted with no fixed seating. There is usually a set of clock faces showing prayer times and there will always be a place set aside for washing before prayer. One wall of the prayer hall, called the **qiblah** wall, has a niche known as the **mihrab** which indicates the direction of Makkah. Near to the mihrab there is a **minbar,** which may be either a high table or a short flight of stairs with a platform at the top. The minbar is used by the Imam when he is addressing the congregation. Men and women worship separately with the men at the front of the prayer hall and the women at the back or upstairs. In many communities they will be entirely separated and most mosques will have separate entrances for men and women with places to put footwear before entering the prayer hall.

The purpose-built mosque usually has a minaret or minar from which the **muezzin** calls Muslims to prayer five times a day. The word minar may be translated as 'the place where light shines'. In past times it was illuminated as a nighttime guide.

ISLAM
Key Stage

KNOWLEDGE AND UNDERSTANDING OF ISLAM (including belief and practice)
'Allah' is the Islamic name for God.
The Oneness of Allah.
Allah has sent guidance through the Qur'an and the Prophets.
Muslims serve Allah in many ways including daily prayer.
Homes and family life including birth and naming ceremonies.
Respect for each other, parents, elders and children.
Stories from the life and traditions of the Prophet Muhammad.
The role of the Mosque.
How people greet each other.
Preparing for festivals and special times.

LEARNING EXPERIENCES
Pupils could:
Share experiences of special occasions in their lives.
Learn that the Islamic name for God is 'Allah'.
Talk about when and how people pray.
Observe wudu and salah and find out where and how they take place.
Listen and respond to stories from the life of the Prophet Muhammad.
Encounter and share in Islamic festivals and find out why they are celebrated.

Listen to Muslims talking about their values.
Meet Muslims.
Distinguish between those things which are made by people and things that belong to the natural world.
Experience and talk about the care of living things.

KEY IDEAS AND QUESTIONS ARISING FROM HUMAN EXPERIENCE
Pupils should be encouraged to think about:
Why we use special names for people.
Why some books are very special.
People who are special to us.
Things we do every day.
How and why we have celebrations.
The importance of doing things together.
What people need for survival.
The natural world and interdependence.

SYMBOLS
The Qur'an and stand.
Hijab.
Subhah.
Prayer carpet.
Compass.
Shalwar.
Kameez.

Scheme of Work: Islam

Glossary

The language of Islam is Arabic. The terms used below are transliterations of simplified versions used by contemporary scholars.

Allah	The Islamic name for God in the Arabic language. Used in preference to the word God, this Arabic term is singular, has no plural, nor is it associated with masculine, feminine or neuter characteristics.
Arafat	A plain, a few kilometres from Makkah, where pilgrims gather to worship, pray and ask for forgiveness. This takes place on the ninth day of the Islamic month of Dhul-Hijjah, the day before Id-ul-Adha.
Hadith	Saying; report; account. The sayings of the Prophet Muhammad, as recounted by his household, progeny and companions. These are a major source of Islamic law. Some Hadith are referred to as Hadith Qudsi (sacred Hadith), having been divinely communicated to the Prophet Muhammad.
Hajj	Annual pilgrimage to Makkah, which each Muslim must undertake at least once in a lifetime if he or she has the health and wealth. A Muslim male who has completed Hajj is called Hajji, and a female, Hajjah.
Hijab	Veil. Often used to describe the head scarf or modest dress worn by women, who are required to cover everything except face and hands in the sight of anyone other than immediate family.
Hijrah	Departure; exit; emigration. The emigration of the Prophet Muhammad from Makkah to Madinah in 622 CE. The Islamic calendar commences from this event.
Imam	Leader. A person who leads the communal prayer, or a founder of an Islamic school of jurisprudence. In Shi'ah Islam, Imam is also the title of Ali (Radhi-Allahu-anhu – may Allah be pleased with him) and his successors.
Jibril	Gabriel. The angel who delivered Allah's messages to His Prophets.
Khadijah	First wife of the Prophet Muhammad. Mother of Fatimah Zahrah (Radhi-Allahu-anhum – may Allah be pleased with them).
Makkah	City where the Prophet Muhammad was born, and where the Ka'bah is located.
Masjid	Place of prostration. Mosque.
Mihrab	Niche or alcove in a mosque wall, indicating the Qiblah – the direction of Makkah, towards which all Muslims face to perform salah.
Mina	Place near Makkah, where pilgrims stay on the 10th, 11th and 12th of Dhul-Hijjah and perform some of the activities of the Hajj.
Minbar	Rostrum; platform; dais. The stand from which the Imam delivers the khutbah or speech in the mosque or praying ground.
Muhammad	Praised. Name of the final Prophet.
Muzdalifah	Place where pilgrims on Hajj stop for a time during the night of the day they spend at Arafat.
Qiblah	Direction which Muslims face when performing salah – towards the Ka'bah.
Qu'ran	That which is read or recited. The Divine Book revealed to the Prophet Muhammad. Allah's final revelation to humankind.
Rak'ah	A unit of salah, made up of recitation, standing, bowing and two prostrations.
Salah	Prescribed communication with, and worship of, Allah, performed under specific conditions, in the manner taught by the Prophet Muhammad, and recited in the Arabic language. The five daily times of salah are fixed by Allah.
Sawm	Fasting from just before dawn until sunset. Abstinence is required from all food and drink (including water) as well as smoking and conjugal relations.
Shahadah	Declaration of faith.
Shi'ah	Followers. Muslims who believe in the Imamah, successorship of Ali (Radhi-Allahu-anhu – may Allah be pleased with him) after the Prophet Muhammad and 11 of his most pious, knowledgeable descendants.
Subhah	String of beads used to count recitations in worship.
Sunnah	Model practices, customs and traditions of the Prophet Muhammad. This is found in both

	Hadith and Sirah.
Sunni	Muslims who believe in the successorship of Abu Bakr, Umar, Uthman and Ali (Radhi-Allahu-anhum – may Allah be pleased with them) after the Prophet Muhammad.
Surah	Division of the Qur'an (114 in all).
Wudu	Ablution before salah.
Zakah	Purification of wealth by payment of annual welfare due. An obligatory act of worship.

Hinduism

Hinduism, as it is called in the West, emerged about five thousand years ago between about 1700 and 1500 BCE, when the North West of India was invaded by the Aryan race who destroyed much of the civilisation of North India and established their own customs, introducing their own gods and a sacred book called the Rig Veda. The Rig Veda contains a large number of 'hymns' addressed to the gods, including Indra, a god of thunder and lightning, war and weather.

The word Hinduism is Persian in origin, meaning 'sindhu' or the river Sind, so 'Hindu' refers to people who live over the Sind. Today the river is called the Indus and over eighty per cent of the population of India are Hindu although of some 700 million Hindus throughout the world about 650 million live outside India. There is a huge diversity of belief and practice but in spite of this there are a number of concepts which are widely accepted by adherents:

- There is one God or One Supreme Spirit, **Brahman.**
- The soul is born many times on earth (reincarnation) through different species from one body to another through the law of **karma** or cause and effect. Most Hindus aim to break the cycle of birth and death (samsara) which occurs when the individual soul (atman) becomes one with the One Soul (Brahman). This breaking of the cycle is called **moksha**
- Moksha, or liberation or freedom, may be attained through spiritual knowledge, meditation (yoga), total love and commitment to God, or through service to humankind without looking for gain.
- God (Brahman) is worshipped in a variety of forms, but especially through Vishnu, Shiva and Shakti.

Shiva

Shiva has many followers. He is a god with great power, representing both creation and destruction, good and evil, simplicity and exuberance, kindliness and fear. He is often portrayed meditating in the Himalayan mountains, seated on an animal skin with his legs crossed in the lotus position.

Shiva is often identified by what he carries: a trident, a snake coiled around his hair or his neck, and prayer beads. Sometimes he is pictured with a fountain emerging from the top-knot in his hair because, according to one story, he allowed the crashing force of the river Ganga (Ganges) to flow through his hair when it descended from heaven to earth. In other images he is shown with a purple neck which is said to be the result of swallowing poison which lodged in his throat. He has four arms. One holds a drum, one a flame of destruction, a third gives a blessing and a fourth points to his feet. It is at Shiva's feet that devotees find happiness and refuge.

Shiva has tremendous energy and, in his form as **Nataraj** or Lord of the Dance, he dances in a circle of flames which represent the cycle of time which has no beginning and no end. He carries the moon on his forehead and beats out the rhythm of the universe on a small drum. His symbol is **lingam** – usually a stone pillar carved in a phallic form as a representation of his masculine creative energy.

He has three eyes with which he is able to perceive the past, present and the future.

Vishnu

Many Hindus in Great Britain worship Vishnu in the form of one of his avatars, usually **Rama,** or **Krishna.** The word avatar means 'one who descends' and avatars are forms which Vishnu took on earth when evil threatened.

Vishnu is depicted as the preserver of the universe and as a personification of goodness and mercy. He wears a jewelled crown and he is often shown seated on a throne or on a serpent. Sometimes he is seen riding Garuda, an eagle-like bird, together with his wife **Lakshmi.** He has four arms and he holds an object in each of them – a conch shell, a discus, a club and a lotus.

Shakti

Some Hindus believe goddesses are the most important objects of worship. The goddess or **devi** is often described as the female form or energy of God. Shiva's wife is one of the goddesses. She has several names. Sometimes she is called **Parvarti**, sometimes **Durga** (a warrior), and sometimes **Kali** when she brings evil, suffering and disease.

Brahma

Brahma is often regarded as the creator of the universe and of other gods. He is usually shown having four heads and faces and four arms. He rides on a goose or a swan. He may carry objects such as a holy book, prayer beads, a water pot or a bow. His wife is **Saraswati**, the goddess of music, arts and literature.

Hanuman

Hanuman is a popular monkey-god, born to the monkey-queen **Anjana**. In the epic story, the **Ramayana**, he helped Rama to save his wife, **Sita**. Hanuman is worshipped as the god of strength and he is respected for his selfless loyalty to Rama.

Ganesha

Ganesha is the son of the goddess Parvarti and the god Shiva. He is an elephant-headed god. He has a jovial nature and he is one of the most popular gods, often found at the doors of temples and homes. People pray to him particularly before they embark on journeys, whilst studying or starting new ventures. He takes the title 'Lord of New Beginnings'.

Ganesha is usually portrayed with four arms and one tusk and he may carry a bowl of sweets, a water lily or a conch shell. He rides on a mouse or a rat!

Several stories tell how Ganesha got his elephant head. In one, his mother, Parvarti, made a figure of a small boy to guard her door whilst she was bathing. When her husband Shiva saw the figure he was upset and cut off the head. Parvarti was so upset that Shiva replaced the head with that of an elephant, the first living creature he saw.

Sacred writings

There are two forms of scriptures. Those which are Revealed are called the Shruti and those which are Remembered are called the Smriti. The **Upanishads** are Shruti and the **Bhagavad Gita** is Smriti, as it is part of the **Mahabharata**, probably the world's longest poem with over two thousand verses. The Bhagavad Gita contains the message that love and devotion to God is the highest form of worship.

Many Hindus do not read the scriptures but become familiar with the stories as they are handed down from generation to generation through the creative and expressive arts.

The Vedas

The Vedic writings are written in Sanskrit. They are divided into a number of groups, the most important of which are Vedas and the Upanishads. The most important of the ancient Vedas is the **Rig Veda**, a collection of over a thousand hymns which were probably used originally in sacrificial worship.

The Upanishads

The Upanishads are a collection of teachings dating between 600 and 200 BCE, generally concerned with the teachings of karma, samsara and moksha and most particularly with the relationship between the individual soul (atman) and the Universal Soul (Brahman).

The Puranas

The Puranas are collections of stories about the gods. Perhaps the most famous are those which tell of Krishna's exploits as a child.

Place of worship

Hindus worship at home and communally in a temple or a **mandir**. Many homes have a shrine with pictures or statues of the gods or deities. Many Hindus will perform a daily ritual in the home, called **puja**, but the ceremony may be carried out in a variety of ways. Flowers, food or incense may be offered to an image or picture.

Meditation or yoga may also be practised. In communal worship there are three main expressions: arti, havan and bhajans.

Arti

Arti is the offering of devotion to God which may take a variety of forms. Usually it includes a tray on which symbols of the five elements are placed. During arti, God is offered prayers, food and light and in turn the worshipper receives God's blessing and then shares **prashad** (sacred or sanctified food) with other people present.

Havan

In the mandir a fire is lit by the priest and ghee or clarified butter or cereal grains are poured into the flame. Havan is a symbol of purity or cleansing before God and the priest may also dip his fingers into water and then touch his ears, nose, mouth, eyes, arms, body and legs before inviting the worshippers to do the same.

Bhajans

Bhajans refers to the singing of devotional hymns or songs. These may be accompanied by cymbals, bells and other musical instruments. Worshippers may also dance.

Festivals

Hinduism has a longer list of festivals than any other religion and the diversity of religious belief and practice is reflected in celebrations, and the timing and length of festivals may vary from place to place.

Holi

Holi is a spring festival lasting from two or three days. In the Western calendar it occurs during February or March. The celebration is sometimes associated with Krishna and stories about a demoness called Holika may be told. Bonfires are usually lit and coconuts may be roasted and offered to God before being shared. The celebration is a joyful one and a time when caste differences are put aside. Sometimes coloured water or paint is sprayed. In Gujarat, babies and young children are often carried around a bonfire, a ritual which symbolises keeping them from harm.

Navaratri

The festival lasts for ten days and occurs during September or October in the Western calendar. In some places the first nine nights are known as Navaratri or Durga Puja and the tenth as **Dassehra.** The celebration occurs throughout India and it is mainly concerned with the worship of the goddess Durga, who is said to have killed the demon Mahishasura on the tenth day. Other goddesses may also be honoured at Navaratri, particularly Saraswati, goddess of music, the arts and literature.

In some parts of northern India the story of Rama from the Ramayana is particularly remembered at this time.

Divali

Divali is celebrated throughout India and it incorporates a wide range of different celebrations. It is usually marked by the lighting of lamps or **divas.** In the Western calendar it falls during October or November. In some places the return of Rama to his kingdom is commemorated. In others it marks the defeat of Mahabali by the dwarf avatar of Vishnu.

Divali marks the end of the financial year and in some places **Lakshmi,** the goddess of wealth, is remembered and divas are lit to help her find her way to homes where it is hoped she will bring good fortune.

HINDUISM
Key Stage

KNOWLEDGE AND UNDERSTANDING OF HINDUISM
(including belief and practice)

Respect for God, other people and all forms of life.
Devotion to God.
Stories recorded in the Hindu scriptures, e.g. Ramayana.
The community: family and other roles.
The universe and the endless cycle of creation, preservation and destruction.
God represented through different names and images.
Reincarnation – the cycle of birth and death.
Hindu traditions: originally an Indian religion; importance of close contact between Hindus in Great Britain and in India; love and loyalty between all family members.
Hindu values: honesty and truthfulness; respect for father and mother.
Hindu worship: festivals; Mandir; home.
Observance of faith: Puja in the home and Mandir.

LEARNING EXPERIENCES

Pupils could:
Look at artefacts and posters depicting Krishna, Rama, Sita.
Find out where India is on a globe or in an atlas.
Visit a Hindu shrine and talk about some of the things in it.
Find out how some Hindu festivals are celebrated.
Listen to stories associated with Hindu festivals.
Find out where their families come from and where they have relatives.
Cook and taste Hindu food.
Watch a film about a Hindu wedding.

KEY IDEAS AND QUESTIONS ARISING FROM HUMAN EXPERIENCE

Pupils should be encouraged to think about:
Family members who live at home and those who live somewhere else.
Special occasions in their own lives.
Groups to which they belong.
Foods which they enjoy on special occasions.
How people have different personalities and how the same person may have different roles in their life.
People they admire.

SYMBOLS

Images/deities.
Fire: havan-kund; bonfires; divas; arti.
Foods: offerings; milk; rice; coconut; sweetmeats; fruit.
Colours.
Janeu.
Mala.

Scheme of Work: Hinduism

Glossary

The terms used are mainly Sanskrit.

Anjana	The monkey queen and mother of Hanuman the monkey warrior.
Arti	Welcoming ceremony in which auspicious articles such as incense and lamps are offered to the deity or to saintly people.
Atman	Self. Can refer to body, mind or soul, depending on context. Ultimately, it refers to the real self, the soul.
Avatar	One who descends. Refers to the descent of a deity, most commonly Vishnu. Sometimes it is translated as incarnation which, although inaccurate, may be the best English word available.
Bhagavad Gita	The Song of the Lord. Spoken by Krishna, this is the most important scripture for most Hindus. Tradition dates it back to 3000 years BCE, though most scholars attribute it to the first millenium BCE. Considered an Upanishad.
Bhajan	Devotional hymn or song.
Brahman	The ultimate reality, or the all-pervading reality; that from which everything emanates, in which it rests and into which it is ultimately dissolved.
Dassehra	Ten days. Also called Vijay Dashami. As is often the case with Hindu festivals, followers may interpret the festival differently, e.g. in connection with Durga (*see* **Navaratri**).
Devi	Female god.
Divali	Festival of lights at the end of one year and beginning of the new year, according to one Hindu calendar.
Durga	Female deity. A form of the goddess Parvarti; wife of Shiva.
Ganesha	A Hindu deity portrayed with an elephant's head – a sign of strength. The deity who removes obstacles.

76

Garuda	The vehicle of Vishnu. An eagle-like bird.
Hanuman	The monkey warrior who faithfully served Rama and Sita. Also called Pavansuta (son of the wind God).
Havan	Also known as Agnihotra. The basis of many Hindu rituals used at weddings and on other ceremonial occasions; the ceremony or act of worship in which offerings of ghee and grains are made into fire.
Havan-kund	The container, usually square or pyramid-shaped, in which the havan fire is burned.
Holi	The festival of colours, celebrated in spring.
Indra	Ancient god of the Aryan race.
Janeu	Sacred thread worn by Hindus who study under a guru.
Kali	Name given to that power of God which delivers justice – often represented by the Goddess Kali (a form of Durga).
Karma	Action. Used of work to refer to the law of cause and effect.
Krishna	Usually considered an avatar of Vishnu. One of the most popular of all Hindu deities in contemporary Britain. His teachings are found in the Bhagavad Gita.
Lingam	Usually a stone pillar carved in a phallic form as a representation of Shiva's masculine energy.
Mahabharata	The Hindu epic that relates the story of the five Pandava princes. It includes the Bhagavad Gita.
Mala	Circle of stringed beads of wood or wool used in meditation.
Mandir	Temple.
Moksha	Ultimate liberation from the process of transmigration, the continuous cycle of birth and death.
Nataraj	Shiva in his form as Lord of the Dance.
Navaratri	The Nine Nights Festival preceding Dassehra, and held in honour of the goddess Durga.
Prashad	Sacred or sanctified food.
Puja	Worship. General term referring to a variety of practices in the home or Mandir.
Purana	Ancient. Part of the Smriti scriptures. Contains many of the well-known stories of Hinduism.
Rakhi	A bracelet, usually made out of silk or cotton, tied to give protection and to strengthen the bond of mutual love.
Rama	The incarnation of the Lord, and hero of the Ramayana (avoid using the variant 'Ram' for obvious reasons).
Ramayana	The Hindu epic that relates the story of Rama and Sita, composed by the sage Valmiki thousands of years ago.
Rig Veda	The first scripture of Hinduism, containing spiritual and scientific knowledge.
Samsara	The world – the place where transmigration (the soul's passage through a series of lives in different species) occurs.
Sanskrit	Sacred language of the Hindu scriptures.
Shakti	Energy or power, especially of a Hindu feminine deity.
Shiva	A Hindu god. The name means 'kindly' or 'auspicious'.
Shruti	That which is remembered. Applicable to Hindu scriptures other than the Vedas.
Sita	The divine consort of Rama.
Smriti	That which is heard. A term specifically applied to the four Vedas, including the Upanishads. Some Hindus believe that Smriti is subservient to Shruti, but other Hindus consider them to have equal importance.
Upanishad	To sit down near. A sacred text based on the teaching of a guru to a disciple. The Upanishads explain the teachings of the Vedas.
Veda	Knowledge. Specifically refers to the four Vedas, though any teaching which is consistent with the conclusions of these scriptures is also accepted as Vedic.
Vishnu	A Hindu god. With Brahmah and Shiva forms the Trimurti.
Yoga	Communion; union of the soul with the Supreme, or a process which promotes that relationship. The English word 'yoke' is derived from yoga.

Sikhism

Adherents of twentieth-century Sikhism include the Amrit Dhari or Khalsa Sikhs and the Sahajdhari Sikhs.

Khalsa males are most commonly recognised by their uncut hair (covered by a turban) and a beard. Sahajdhari Sikhs cut their hair and may not observe the 5Ks and other tenets of the faith.

The founder of Sikhism was **Guru Nanak** who lived in the fifteenth century and was born into a Hindu family. The word Sikh means 'disciple'. Nanak rejected the caste system and idolatry and taught that one God should be worshipped; that all humankind are equal and that people should devote themselves to good actions and to God. Guru Nanak established the idea of a **langar** or free kitchen where people could eat regardless of race or creed.

When Guru Nanak died in 1539 his teaching was continued by the second Guru **Angad**, who placed emphasis on equality and education. The third Guru, **Amar Das**, reinforced previous teaching concerning equality. The fourth Guru, **Ram Das,** founded the holy city of Amritsar and began the building of the **Golden Temple** which was continued by his successor, **Guru Arjan**, in 1589. Guru Arjan also wrote many sacred hymns and he collected these together with those of former Gurus in a holy book called the **Adi Granth** (or Guru Granth Sahib), which was installed in the Golden Temple. Guru Arjan was the first Guru to be born a Sikh and his reign marks the fullest establishment of Sikhism. Guru Arjan was also the first Sikh martyr. His successor was his son Guru **Har-Gobind** who became Guru when he was only eleven years old.

Guru Har-Gobind chose to wear two swords as symbols of the political and spiritual authority of the Gurus and he encouraged community and religious matters to be discussed in the temples. The Guru also kept a small army which was distinguished by a pennant which later became the Sikh 'flag' or **nishan sahib**. The seventh Guru, **Har Rai**, was the grandson of Guru Har-Gobind but less of a military figure than his grandfather. He is remembered for his interest in herbs and medicine and was succeeded by his youngest son Guru **Har Krishan** at the age of five. Unfortunately Guru Har Krishan contracted smallpox at the age of eight whilst helping victims of the disease and died, but not before he had nominated his successor Guru **Tegh Bahadur**. The name Tegh Bahadur means 'brave sword'. In Guru Tegh Bahadur's time, Moghul rulers wanted to forcibly convert Hindu subjects to Islam, a policy which Guru Tegh Bahadur condemned. Eventually he was arrested and four of his companions were executed for refusing to become Muslims. The Guru was asked to convert to Islam but he refused and was put to death. He is revered as one who died protecting Sikhism.

Guru **Gobind Singh** succeeded his father Guru Tegh Bahadur, and he is the most loved and admired of all the Gurus save for Guru Nanak. He was a poet and linguist, and a book which may contain some of his poems, called the **Dasam Granth**, is still venerated today. He performed two important religious acts in his life which are of great significance to Sikhism.

Just before he died in October 1708 Guru Gobind Singh took five coins and a coconut and placed them before a copy of the Guru Granth Sahib. (This was the way a new Guru was designated.) Therefore the guidance contained in the Guru Granth Sahib was his successor.

The Pure Ones

On **Baisakhi** day in 1699 thousands of Sikhs had gathered to pay homage to Guru Gobind Singh. He asked if anyone would give his life for him. A man followed the Guru into a tent and the sound of a sword was heard. When Guru Gobind Singh reappeared his sword was dripping with blood and he asked for another volunteer. Another man offered himself, and again he was taken into the tent where more noises were heard. The request was made five times and each time a volunteer came forward. Suddenly the Guru reappeared, followed by the five men. The Guru explained he had carried out the exercise to demonstrate the need for unity and brotherhood. The five volunteers were named the five 'beloved ones' and they were given **amrit** or sugared water which had been stirred with a steel sword. This was the foundation of the **Khalsa** or the 'Pure Ones'.

Today, Khalsa Sikhs still undergo a special initiation ceremony (**amrit samskar**) where they promise to honour and abide by the rules of Sikhism by wearing the 5Ks.

Sacred writings

The Sikh holy book is the **Guru Granth Sahib**. The opening words of the book contain the **Mool Mantar** which embodies the basic beliefs of Sikh belief:

There is one God,
Eternal Truth is God's name,
Creator of all things,
Fearless and without hatred,
Timeless and formless,

Beyond birth and death,
Self-enlightened
By the grace of the Guru God is known.

The Guru Granth Sahib is the focal point of all Sikh worship and is treated with great reverence and respect. It is usually kept under a **palki** or canopy and read from a **manji** or dais. The **granthi** or reader reverently moves a **chauri** over the pages. In Amritsar continuous readings of the Guru Granth Sahib take place.

Place of worship

The Sikh place of worship is called the **gurdwara**, a word which means 'the door of the Guru'. It is a name given to any place where a copy of the Guru Granth Sahib is kept. This may be a purpose-built place or a private house. Central to worship are the sacred scriptures but the gurdwara is also a social centre where a **langar** or free kitchen provides food for all people regardless of race or creed.

Worship is often flexible and informal and there is usually a group of musicians or singers who sit near the Guru Granth Sahib and sing verses or **shabads** from the scriptures. The congregation will remove their shoes before entering the prayer room, which is carpeted so the congregation can sit on the floor. Offerings of food and money may be made and on special occasions Sikhs may offer a **romalla** or cover for the Guru Granth Sahib. Women generally sit to the left of the holy book and men to the right, taking care not to point their feet towards the Guru Granth Sahib.

There is no regular holy day in Sikhism but in Britain it is often Sunday. Services may vary between an hour and several hours and all will end with a prayer called **Ardas** which is in three parts. Firstly there is a commemoration of God and the Gurus. Secondly the congregation are asked to think about the Guru Granth Sahib and to remember faithful Sikhs such as those who gave their lives for their faith. In addition, the four 'seats

---

A SPECIAL PLACE THE GURDWARA

The gurdwara is like home. Lots of my friends go there. In the entrance hall we take off our shoes. This makes it even more like home! We cover our heads and we go to the prayer room where our holy book the Guru Granth Sahib is placed. Once I helped to clean all the shoes outside the prayer hall. It took all morning.

'When my sister got married we put on our new ·clothes and went to the gurdwara. The groom was at the front of the prayer hall and my sister was at the back with lots of women looking after her. After shabads and a talk about marriage my sister and the groom walked around the prayer hall four times. Each time it got more exciting because at the end they were married. We threw flower petals over them'.

'We were all excited in my family when we got a baby brother. When he came home from hospital we all got dressed in our best clothes and we took him to the gurdwara to say "thank you" to God. The Guru Granth Sahib was opened and the first letter of the shabad on the left of the page was a 'p'. My parents had to choose a name beginning with that letter. They called my brother Pavan.

'When my little sister was born my family bought all the food for the langar. I helped with the shopping too. There were sacks of potatoes, vegetables, flour, sugar, drums of ghee and all sorts of other things. The night before we took my sister to the gurdwara our friends helped us to prepare the food for 300 people which took a long time. My favourite food is semolina halva. Here is the recipe my grandma makes:

SEMOLINA HALVA

475 ml water
140 g sugar
4 tsp vegetable oil or ghee
Half teaspoon crushed cardamom seeds
250 g semolina
20 g chopped blanched almonds
25 g sultanas

METHOD
Boil the water. Heat the oil or ghee until it is runny. Fry the semolina in the oil or ghee until it is golden brown. Stir in the almonds, cardamom seeds and the sultanas. Pour in the sugared water and cook over a low heat for 5 minutes.

First published in *RESPECT*, the journal of the RE and Special Needs Network

of authority' in India are remembered. The final part is a request for God's blessing on all humanity. Members of the congregation often respond to the petitions with the words 'Waheguru' which may be translated as 'wonderful Lord'.

At the end of the service a member of the congregation stirs a mixture of semolina, butter and sugar, known as **karah parshad**. This is distributed to everyone present as a symbol of God's blessing and the equality of all humankind.

Sikh belief

The basis of Sikh belief is:

- God is One; God is the **Supreme Truth**; the **Ultimate Reality** and the **Creator** of all things.
- Humankind contain a 'spark' of Godliness.
- Humankind should seek to commune with God and to accept his will.
- Sikhs should strive for self-control, forgiveness, contentment, love of God, humility, hard work, sharing profit and helping the less able and the community.

Sikhism also teaches that the soul of a person is not predestined. What a person does in this life, good or bad, will affect their soul. If a person persists in evil actions they will find themselves in an endless cycle of birth and death. God is merciful, however, and offers deliverance from bad deeds.

The 5Ks or Panj kakke

Sikhs are encouraged to be formally confirmed into their faith through an initiation ceremony known as **Amrit**. During Amrit Sikhs promise to honour and abide by the 5Ks.

SIKHISM
Key Stage

KNOWLEDGE AND UNDERSTANDING OF SIKHISM (including belief and practice)
There is one God who is the Creator.
All humans are equal before God.
Ceremonies: e.g. naming, marriage, turban-tying.
Celebrations: e.g. birthdays of Guru Nanak, Guru Gobind Singh: Baisakhi.
The lives of the Gurus.
The Guru Granth Sahib – its care in the Gurdwara.
Worship – led by the Granthi. Consists of: kirtan; ardas; langar.

LEARNING EXPERIENCES
Pupils could:
Hear Sikhs talking about themselves and their faith.
Listen to stories about Guru Nanak and other Gurus.
Observe a Sikh tying his turban.
Find out about the birthday of Guru Nanak and how it is celebrated.
Look at pictures or a video of the Golden temple and find out where Amritsar is on a map.
Listen to the story of Baisakhi.
Share ideas about the importance of the names and look up their own names in a dictionary of first names.
Visit a Gurdwara and identify expressions of Sikh belief and practice.
Make a poster explaining the 5 Ks.
Design their own symbol(s) to express something about themselves.

KEY IDEAS AND QUESTIONS ARISING FROM HUMAN EXPERIENCE
Pupils should be encouraged to think about:
Times when it is easy to share and times when it is difficult.
Their own families and the activities which they enjoy.
Signs of belonging, e.g. uniforms, badges, symbols.
Ways in which people demonstrate respect, and how it feels to be respected.
Feelings which are evoked when visiting a place of worship.
The importance of community meals – meals which are special.
Books which are special to them.

SYMBOLS
The 5 Ks: kachera; kangha; kara; kesh; kirpan.
Karah parshad.
Khanda.
Nishan Sahib.

Scheme of Work: Sikhism

- **Kesh** – to wear body hair uncut.
- **Kachera** – to wear loose underwear(shorts) as a symbol of self discipline.
- **Kangha** – a comb which fastens hair beneath the turban and is a symbol of cleanliness.
- **Kara** – a steel band worn on the right wrist which symbolises the unbreakable link with the faith.
- **Kirpan** – a sword worn to symbolise a duty to fight against evil.

Festivals

Baisakhi

In Punjab Baisakhi is New Year's Day (13th or 14th April in the Western calendar) and also the day on which Guru Gobind Singh instituted the Khalsa in 1699 CE. It is a popular time for Sikhs to be initiated into the faith. Baisakhi is also a time when the Sikh nation is remembered and political speeches may take place. In Amritsar the celebration is marked by an animal fair or livestock market.

Diwali

Diwali is a festival celebrated throughout India. It marks the end of the rainy season and the beginning of autumn. Three events are particularly called to mind at the celebration. Firstly, Sikhs remember it as the time of the year when Guru Ram Das laid the foundations of the city of Amritsar. Secondly, it also marks the time when Guru Har-Gobind was released from imprisonment. Thirdly Sikhs remember that in 1738 CE the custodian of the Golden Temple was martyred at Diwali. In most cases the festival is marked by firework displays and community festivities.

Hola Mohalla

Hola Mohalla was first celebrated after the formation of the Khalsa in 1700 CE. The name Hola Mohalla may be translated as 'attack and place of attack'. The festival marks the beginning of the spring and Anandapur is often the centre of the festivities, where wrestling matches and fencing tournaments take place. Funfairs are popular.

Gurpurbs

In addition to these three festivals Sikhs also observe celebrations and commemorations called gurpurbs. The word gurpurb means 'festival connected with the Guru' and often continuous readings of the Guru Granth Sahib will take place. The holy book may be taken in procession through a town or village accompanied by five men representing the five **panj pyares** or five brave people prepared to die for their faith on Baisakhi day.

The four most important gurpurbs are: **Guru Nanak's birthday** (November in the Western calendar); **Guru Gobind Singh's birthday** (December or January in the Western calendar); the **Martyrdom of Guru Arjan Dev** (May or June in the Western calendar); the **Martyrdom of Guru Tegh Bahadur** (December in the Western calendar).

Glossary

The terms used are based on the Punjabi language.

Adi Granth	The holy book or Guru Granth Sahib.
Amrit	Nectar. Sanctified liquid made of sugar and water, used in initiation ceremonies.
Ardas	Prayer. The formal prayer offered at most religious acts.
Baisakhi	A major Sikh festival celebrating the formation of the Khalsa, 1699 CE.
Dasam Granth	Collection of compositions, some of which are attributed to the tenth Sikh Guru, compiled some years after his death.
The Five Ks	(*See* Panj kakke).
Granthi	Reader of the Guru Granth Sahib, who officiates at ceremonies.
Gurdwara	Sikh place of worship. Literally the 'doorway to the Guru'.
Gurpurb	A Guru's anniversary (birth or death). Also used for other anniversaries, e.g. the installation of the Adi Granth, 1604 CE.

Guru Gobind Singh	Tenth Sikh Guru. It is important to note that the title 'Guru' must be used with all the Gurus' names. Sikhs usually use further terms of respect, e.g. Guru Gobind Singh Ji or Guru Nanak Dev Ji.
Guru Granth Sahib	Primal collection of Sikh scriptures, compiled by Guru Arjan and given its final form by Guru Gobind Singh.
Guru Nanak	The first Guru and the founder of the Sikh faith (1469-1539).
Kachera	Traditional underwear/shorts. One of the 5 K's (*see* Panj kakke).
Kangha	Comb worn in the hair. One of the 5 K's (see panj kakke).
Kara	Steel band worn on the right wrist. One of the 5 K's (*see* Panj kakke).
Karah parshad	Sanctified food distributed at Sikh ceremonies.
Kesh	Uncut hair. One of the 5 K's (*see* Panj kakke).
Khalsa	The community of the pure. The Sikh community.
Khanda	Double-edged sword used in the initiation ceremony. Also used as the emblem on the Sikh flag.
Kirpan	Sword. One of the 5 K's (*see* Panj kakke). 'Dagger' should be avoided.
Kirtan	Devotional singing of the compositions found in the Guru Granth Sahib.
Langar	Guru's kitchen. The gurdwara dining hall and the food served in it.
Mool Mantar	Basic teaching; essential teaching. The basic statement of belief at the beginning of the Guru Granth Sahib.
Nishan Sahib	Sikh flag flown at gurdwaras.
Palki	A canopy or covering over the Guru Granth Sahib.
Panj kakke	The 5 K's. The symbols of Sikhism worn by Sikhs.
Panj pyares	The five beloved ones. Those first initiated into the Khalsa; those who perform the rite today.
Romalla	An embroidered cover for the Guru Granth Sahib.
Shabad	Word. Hymn from the Guru Granth Sahib; the divine word.

Buddhism

Buddhism shares some basic roots and ideas with Hinduism but differs in many important teachings. The religion began with the experience of Siddhartha Gautama who was born in North East India between the sixth and the fourth century BCE. The precise time is unknown. Traditionally Siddhartha Gautama is thought to have been the son of a wealthy king . At the age of twenty it is said that he encountered suffering, old-age, sickness and death for the first time. He also saw a serene holy man who impressed him. Siddhartha Gautama left his wife and baby son and began to search for a way to freedom from the endless cycle of birth, suffering and death. Eventually through meditation he gained the understanding for which he had been looking and shared his insights with others over a period of about forty years. Although Siddhartha Gautama is regarded by Buddhists as the supreme example, it is important to understand that he is not regarded as a god. Buddhism is the path to liberation from the bondage of greed, anger and delusion which is within the reach of all people.

There are two major divisions within Buddhism today: Theravada Buddhism and Mahayana Buddhism.

Theravada Buddhism

Theravada Buddhism is found in Sri Lanka, Thailand, Laos, Burma, Kampuchea and the West. It is the most conservative form of Buddhism. The word Theravada means 'Way of the Elders' and its basic scriptures are called the **Pali Canon**. The main beliefs are expressed in The Four Noble Truths of the Buddha and The Noble Eightfold Path.

Mahayana Buddhism

Mahayana Buddhism (meaning 'Great Way' or 'Great Vehicle') is followed by the majority of Buddhists and adherents are found in Nepal, Tibet, Japan, Korea, China and the West. It includes Zen and Pure Land Buddhism. Mahayana Buddhism welcomes a variety of practices which may lead to and express wisdom and compassion. It includes many philosophies, beliefs and local customs in its path. In Nepal, for example, the faith is combined with Hindu practices. However, it shares with Theravada the emphasis on putting aside cravings and desires as a means to enlightenment and basic teachings such as the Noble Truths and the Noble Eightfold Path. All Buddhists also believe that all beings will eventually attain **Nirvana.**

The Four Noble Truths

The First Noble Truth is the truth of 'suffering ' or duhkha (often translated as unsatisfactoriness). The word duhkha describes all that is unsatisfactory including what is impermanent, birth, decay, sorrow, sickness and death.

The Second Noble Truth is a 'craving or desire' which leads to tension and suffering. Sometimes the word 'grasping' is used instead.

The Third Noble Truth teaches that suffering ends when desire ends. Therefore if a person rids themself of desire then freedom from suffering and from the chain of re-birth is possible.

The Fourth Noble Truth is a practical way of dealing with craving or desire known as 'The Noble Eightfold Path'.

The Noble Eightfold Path

This is a description of eight stages in the path to the ending of desire and finding peace and detachment. There are three main areas: morality, meditation and wisdom.

Right views

The four truths of the Buddha are recommended and taught as stages in the path to be lived experientially. They are suggested as appropriate for the goal to be reached.

Right thought

People should not merely resolve to think good things but should also be concerned with where they direct their thoughts, striving to be free from selfish desires and ill will towards others.

Right speech

The Buddha taught that words have consequences. Therefore speech should always avoid harsh words and be truthful.

Right action

Deeds as well as words have consequences. Killing, taking what is not given and sexual misconduct are discouraged by Buddhists. Eventually good deeds enable enlightenment.

Right livelihood

A person should earn their living in an occupation which is not luxurious and which does not harm other people.

Right effort

The Buddhist must be constantly making an effort to put away evil desires and to develop inner virtues.

Right awareness

Buddhist teaching recommends a person should direct their whole attention towards what they are doing.

Right meditation

This refers to an ability to concentrate the mind totally during meditation.

Festivals

Asala or Dhammacakka Day

This commemorates the fi teaching by the Buddha at Sarnath where he taught the Middle way, the Noble Eightfold Path and the Fou Noble Truths.

Kathina

The festival occurs at the end of the three-month Rains Retreat in Theravada Buddhism when lay members of the community present monks with new robes.

Wesak

A Theravada festival commemorating the birth, enlightenment and death of the Buddha, normally in May or June in the Western calendar.

New Year

A New Year festival is celebrated in Sri Lanka, Tibet and Japan but the dates vary because different calendars are followed, e.g. Japan follows the Western calendar.

Places of worship

Shrines may vary from very simple to elaborate. Many Buddhists will have a shrine in their home. Although the Buddha is not considered to be a god an image is often placed in an elevated position in a shrine as a mark of respect. Buddhists will remove their shoes before entering a shrine and they will often offer gifts of flowers, food, incense or light. In return monks give teaching. There may be a **bodhi tree** and **stupas** (mounds containing relics) which also act as a focus of attention. Mahayana shrines often have more pictures and images and hangings than Theravada shrines. Zen (Mahayana shrines) sometimes have a meditation garden of raked sand attached to them which helps create a sense of stillness and calm for the meditator.

Sacred writings

The sacred writings of Theravada Buddhism are the **Pali Canon**, which are also known as **Tripitaka**, meaning 'three baskets' of texts. These are concerned with the rules of the monastic life, the teaching or 'word' of the Buddha, and philosophical and psychological teachings in a more abstract form. Mahayana scriptures are also held to contain the teachings of Siddhartha Gautama. They include the **Diamond Sutra**, the **Heart Sutra**, and **Lotus Sutra**.

BUDDHISM
Key Stage

KNOWLEDGE AND UNDERSTANDING OF BUDDHISM (including belief and practice)
Stories from the life of Buddha which show: concern for others; suffering.
Buddhist teaching: compassion; respect for all living things; importance of generosity; kindness; truth; and patience.
Respect and gratitude of children towards adults; duties of adults towards children.
Awareness: the importance of reflection and meditation; being aware of how thoughts and feelings lead to actions.
The community: lay persons; monks; nuns.
The Five Moral Precepts.
The Four Noble Truths.
The Noble Eightfold Path.

LEARNING EXPERIENCES
Pupils could:
Hear stories about the life of Siddhartha Gautama.
Look at and examine images of the Buddha.
Watch a video about Buddhist celebrations, e.g. festivals which celebrate the Buddha's birth, enlightenment and passing away.
Share feelings about the importance of families and friends.
Make a poster describing the Noble Eightfold Path.

KEY IDEAS AND QUESTIONS ARISING FROM HUMAN EXPERIENCE
Pupils should be encouraged to think about:
How it feels when they are respected and treated kindly.
How it feels when they are hurt and frightened.
What it would be like for a prince today to give up all that he owned.
The value of living in a community, e.g. school.
The need for rules in everyday life.

SYMBOLS
Images of the Buddha.
The lotus flower.
The wheel.
The Bodhi tree.

Scheme of Work: Buddhism

Glossary

As Buddhism spread throughout the East, it became expressed in many languages. There is no preferred form. Sanskrit terms are used throughout the text below.

Bodhi tree	The tree (ficus religiosa) under which the Buddha realised Enlightenment. It is known as the Tree of Wisdom.
Duhkha	Suffering; ill; unsatisfactoriness; imperfection. The nature of existence according to the first Noble Truth.
Nirvana	Blowing out of the fires of greed, hatred and ignorance and the state of secure, perfect peace that follows. A key Buddhist term.
Pali Canon	The Sacred writings of Theravada Buddhism.

Siddhartha Gautama	Wish fulfilled. The personal name of the historical Buddha.
Sutra	Text – the word of the Buddha.
Theravada	Way of the elders. A principal school of Buddhism, established in Sri Lanka and South East Asia. Also found in the West.
Tripitaka	Three baskets. A threefold collection of texts (Vinaya, Sutta, Abhidamma).
Wesak	Buddha Day. Name of a festival and a month. On the full moon of Wesak (in May or June), the birth, Enlightenment and passing away of the Buddha took place, although some schools celebrate only the birth at this time, e.g. Zen.
Zen	(Japanese) Meditation. Derived from the Sanskrit 'dhyana'. A school of Mahayana Buddhism that developed in China and Japan.

Chinese Culture

There are three main religions or philosophical systems recognised in China: Buddhism, Taoism and Confucianism. Each of the systems has made a contribution to the beliefs, rites and customs of the Chinese people. However, beyond the philosophical systems is also an ancient set of beliefs which are deeply-rooted in the culture of the Chinese people. These beliefs centre on Ancestor-worship, which holds that good and malevolent ghosts, gods, spirits and demons continually interact with the everyday living world.

The old-style Chinese calendar said to have been devised by the legendary Yellow Emperor Huang Ti is a lunar one made up of twelve lunar months of twenty nine or thirty days each. Each year is dominated by one of twelve animals of the zodiac who are believed to posses individual characteristics which influence the course of events.

The Gregorian calendar or Western calendar was introduced in 1912 but this has not led to the abandonment of the traditional Chinese system of time reckoning. Indeed many Chinese calendars incorporate the lunar, the Chinese solar and the western solar calendar systems.

Perhaps the most important of the Chinese festivals is **Yuan Tan** or **Chinese New Year,** which falls on the first day of the first lunar month of the year.

Although Chinese New Year is not a religious festival many schools celebrate the occasion. Therefore an outline of the festival is included within Chinese Culture. Colleagues are urged to emphasise the cultural origins and, if the topic is chosen, to include it within general curriculum themes such as homes, families and lifestyles and not as a religious festival.

Chinese New Year

For many people of Chinese origin, the festival of Yuan Tan or Chinese New Year is an opportunity to celebrate ancient traditions. The festival begins on the twenty third day of the twelfth moon when the Kitchen God, whose duty it is to watch over families, ascends to heaven to report on the conduct of each person throughout the year.

Whilst the Kitchen God is away, families thoroughly clean their homes and some will newly paint doors and windows for the occasion. New clothes are purchased, debts cleared and disagreements resolved. Often, large pictures or images of gate gods, dressed in armour and carrying weapons, are placed by the entrances to houses to frighten off evil spirits which are said to walk the earth just before the New Year. Red banners may also be hung on windows and gates as a deterrent to the spirits.

On New Year's Eve a moyiefa tree with yellow blossom is brought into homes as a symbol of a new start. A special meal is prepared and candles and incense sticks are lit to welcome back the Kitchen God and in remembrance of family members who have died or who are unable to be present. After sharing food, games are played until just before midnight. Card games are particulary popular. At midnight people leave their homes and congregate in streets where bonfires are lit and fire crackers are let off to frighten away any remaining demons. Sometimes a dragon procession visits houses as a symbol of good fortune and money is offered to the people inside the dragon as an incentive for them to visit neighbouring houses. The celebrations continue throughout the night until the dawn of New Year's Day when new clothes are put on and homes become the focal point for festivities. Newly minted money in red envelopes is given to children and unmarried persons to encourage good fortune throughout the year ahead. Many of the games played include gambling, fortunes are told and people exchange greetings of happiness and long life.

The festival continues for fifteen days but it is the first three days and the last day which are most important. People visit one another in their homes, often taking gifts of sweets, biscuits and crystallised or fresh fruits. On the second day

CHINESE NEW YEAR
Key Stage

KNOWLEDGE AND UNDERSTANDING OF CHINESE CULTURE (including belief and practice)

The importance of calendars.
The importance of special times to the Chinese community.
Astrology.
Moon festivals.
Stories from ancient Chinese traditions.
The balance between good and evil.
Fire and the elements.
Good fortune, long life and happiness.

LEARNING EXPERIENCES

Pupils could:
Find out which sign of the Chinese zodiac they were born under.
Look at and handle artefacts from Chinese traditions.
Share feelings about values which might be important to them, e.g. goodness, long life.
Hear the story of the animals at Chinese New Year.
Talk about important figures in their own lives. especially parents/carers.
Think about how their own home is prepared for a special occasion.
Dress up in Chinese clothes.
Share a Chinese meal.
Bake fortune cookies.

KEY IDEAS AND QUESTIONS ARISING FROM HUMAN EXPERIENCE

Pupils should be encouraged to think about:
New beginnings – making a fresh start.
How they are kept safe/from harm.
How we remember people when they are absent.
What it is like to belong to group.
How people express their different personalities.
Meals and celebrations which are special to them.
Giving and receiving gifts.

SYMBOLS

Colours: especially red and gold.
Moyiefa tree.
Candles and incense sticks.
Bonfires.
Signs of the Chinese zodiac.
Lanterns.
Special foods: noodles; rice; fortune cookies; dumplings.

---

daughters may visit their parents taking presents such as cake and mandarin oranges.

The festivities conclude with the Lantern Festival on the first full moon. Lanterns decorate homes and streets and once again food is shared and the future is looked forward to as an opportunity for wealth and happiness.

Sensory learning experiences

- Touch the smooth surface of the lacquer which coats some of the Chinese objects.
- Trace the shape of the Chinese writing with your fingers.
- Enjoy the feel of a fan wafting air around your body.
- Feel the surface of a semi-folded fan.
- Help to make Chinese lanterns and enjoy them as they hang in the classroom.
- Enjoy the texture of a piece of Chinese silk and look at the different shades of colour within the fabric.

The cycle of the years

The twelve years of the animals (see story) form a repeated cycle. Depending upon the name of the year a person is born in, they are said to show certain characteristics. An ancient Chinese saying declares, "This is the animal which hides in your heart."

The Year of the Rat

People born under this sign are lively, friendly, happy and charming. They are sociable, but tend to be excitable. A child born during the day is likely to have a rich easy life, for rats are supposed to sleep by day and to hunt by night. On the other hand, a child born at night may expect to have to work hard for a living.

The Year of the Ox

A child born in this year is dependable and trustworthy, particular and non-conformist. They are likely to be blessed with many children and to have a happy and fruitful life.

The Year of the Tiger

Tigers are powerful, audacious and passionate. A child born in this year is likely to be unpredictable and rebellious, but they are loyal and good providers for their family. The tigress is a shrewd manager.

THE STORY OF THE NEW YEAR ANIMALS

The following story about twelve animals who argued that each year of the Chinese calendar should be given a name is often told to children at Chinese New Year.

"The year should be named after me," said the dog. "It should be called the Year of the Dog."

The monkey disagreed. "No," he said, "it must be the Year of the Monkey." "No, no," shouted the dragon. "Surely it should be named after me. It must be called The Year of the Dragon."

As the animals argued the gods listened and they told the animals to stop. They said the way to decide the name of the year would be for all the creatures to have a race across a river. The winner would have the year dedicated to them. The animals lined up on the river bank, jumped off and swam as fast as they could to the opposite bank. The ox was very strong and soon he was ahead of all the others. But the rat was clever. He grabbed the tail of the ox and pulled himself onto the animal's back. The ox did not know he was there!

Just before the ox reached the other side of the river the rat jumped off his back onto the grass. He shouted, "Hooray, I am first."

The ox was amazed but the rat only laughed. The gods laughed too and said, "The rat is the winner. We will call this year the Year of the Rat. The ox was second, so next year will be the Year of the Ox."

All the other animals finished the race. The tiger was third; the hare was fourth; the dragon was fifth; the snake sixth; the horse seventh; the ram eighth, the monkey ninth; the cockerel was tenth; the dog eleventh and the pig was last. The gods decided each year would be named after one of the animals and the creatures didn't argue any more. They were all happy, especially the rat because he had won the race!

The Year of the Hare

A person born under this sign is likely to be blessed with many children. They are likely to have a long, happy and peaceful life. Hares are gentle, aware of beauty around them, polite and considerate.

The Year of the Dragon

Dragons are blessed with energy and strength. A child born in this year will have high ambitions and lead a very full life. They will usually be fond of night-time. They do not like sudden decisions and change.

The Year of the Snake

Snakes are wise, softly spoken and prim, capable of sound judgements and deep thoughts. A child born in this year will be conscientious and persistent.

The Year of the Horse

The horse is strong, talkative and friendly with an attractive personality, showing great sensitivity towards other people. A child born in this year is likely to fall in and out of love easily.

The Year of the Ram

The ram is said to be proud. He is a good leader with strong instincts to help humankind. A child born in this year will be sympathetic but often pessimistic.

The Year of the Monkey

This animal is agile and has quick movements and a lively mind. A child born in this year will be curious and highly observant, charming but deceitful. They will not mind their own business. They will however be a good problem solver and are likely to be successful in learning. They would be a loving parent.

The Year of the Cockerel

The cockerel tends to be aggressive, proud and cocksure. There are two types of cockerel – one who talks continuously in a loud, lively and amusing manner, and the other who is inclined to stare with cold, clear eyes. A child born in this year is likely to be handsome and industrious.

The Year of the Dog

Dogs are likeable and make loyal friends. They are honest, sincere, persistent and intelligent. A child born in this year will insist on fairness and justice. They will be very attractive to the opposite sex.

The Year of the Pig

Pigs are honest and brave. A child born in this year is likely to cope well with the difficulties of life. They will never bear grudges and will know when to apologise. Pigs are intelligent and caring and make excellent parents.

Chinese New Year

1. Lanterns
2. Banner with Good Luck! greeting
3. Kitchen god
4. Rice and chop sticks
5. Fan
6. Greetings cards
7. Dragon
8. Kitchen god kite
9. Banner with Happy New Year! greeting

CHAPTER 9

Developing Children's Awareness of Human Experience Through Story

From an historical point of view, story has always been held in high esteem. Plato applauded it, and the greatest teachers, including Jesus, acknowledged the worth of stories as aids to understanding what was being taught. Today, there is yet again a growing awareness of the value of fiction, sacred writings and prose in Religious Education. All children, regardless of their background, enter into a heritage which includes stories, poems, words, expressions, phrases, rhymes and jingles. And the religions of the world provide us with a rich storehouse of literature.

Most adults can recall favourite books which made a strong impression on them in childhood and the affection with which these are remembered is an indication of their value. Through fictional characters people gain insight into themselves and their quest for personal identity. The sharing of a good story has the capacity to entertain and to evoke a response. In the context of Religious Education, stories which possess these qualities can also fulfil some of the following:

- **Information giving:** pupils can learn more about people, events and places.
- **Question raising:** many stories will prompt children to ask questions and to reflect on ideas, beliefs and values.
- **Evoking sensitivity:** an opportunity is provided to awaken an awareness of issues, needs and feelings.
- **Creative imagination:** windows can be opened on to another world which can be explored.
- **Cognitive development:** ideas and information can be introduced and explored as a pre-requisite to understanding concepts and knowledge.

The following sections list picture and story books which have been chosen to help pupils explore questions and dilemmas arising from human experience. The list is not exhaustive and schools are urged to select titles which reflect the family backgrounds of life experiences of the children in their care. Most of the books are still in print. Others have been selected according to titles most readily available from public libraries, professional development centres and Religious Education resource centres in England and Wales.

Three activity outlines are also included which develop themes of New Beginnings, Death and Dying, and Journeys.

Human Experience

Myself and relationships
Key stage 1
Wilfred Gordon, McDonald Partridge M Fox & J Vivas (Picture Puffin)
Big Sister and Little Sister C Zolotow (Piccolo Picture Books)
Noisy Nora R Wells (Picture Lions)
Are We Nearly There? L Baum (Magnet)
Ben's Baby M Foreman (Red Fox)
A Baby Sister for Frances R Hoban (Faber)
Where Did You Come From? J Powell (Wayland)
Who Are You? J Powell (Wayland)

Ourselves and our homes

Peter's Chair E Keats (Bodley Head)
From Me to You P Rogers (Orchard Books)
Changing Baby Hollie ILEA (Phototalk Books)
Jenny's Baby Brother P Smith (Collins)
Janine and the New Baby I Thomas (Andre Deutsch)
The Clown of God T de Paola (Methuen)
A New Baby T Berger (Macdonald)
The New Baby K Petty (Franklin Watts)
My Big Brother R Coote (Firefly)
Tall Inside J Richardson (Puffin)
I Like Me N Carlson (Puffin)
Grannies and Grandads S Perry (A & C Black)
Brothers and Sisters S Perry (A & C Black)
Jafta H Lewin (Hamish Hamilton)

Key Stage 2
Willy and Hugh A Brown (Julia McRea Books)
The Boy and the Swan C Storr (Deutsch)
Family Tree K Webb (Hamish Hamilton)
The Twelfth Day of July J Lingard (Puffin/Hamish Hamilton)
Joseph's Yard C Keeping (OUP)
The Pinballs B Byers (Bodley Head/Puffin)
Red Sky in the Morning E Laird (Puffin)
Thunder and Lightning J Mark (Puffin)
Gaffer Sampson's Luck J Paton Walsh (Puffin)
The Velveteen Rabbit M Williams (Heinemann/Carousel)
Who Are Your Family? J Powell (Wayland)
Who Are Your Friends? J Powell (Wayland)
Yourself M Pollard (Wayland)

Divorce/single parents/new families
Key Stage 1
The Not-So-Wicked Stepmother L Boyd (Puffin)

The Twig Thing J Mark (Puffin)
I Have Two Homes Althea (Dinosaur)
Where Has Daddy Gone? T Osman (Heinemann)
The Christmas Train I Gantschev (Kestrel)
My Dad G Thompson (Longman)
My Daddy S Boothroyd (Hodder & Stoughton)
My Mother's Getting Married J Drescher (Methuen)

Key Stage 2
Family Saturday M Newman (Hamish Hamilton)
Marmalade, Jet and the Finnies E Wignell (Hamish Hamilton)
Lottie and Lisa E Kastner (Puffin)
Keeping Henry N Bawden (Puffin)
Mr Berry's Ice Cream Parlour J Zabel (Puffin)
Children Don't Divorce R Stones (Dinosaur)
Splitting Up K Petty et al (Franklin Watts)
Mum, Will Dad Ever Come Back? P Hogan (Blackwell)
Adoption K Bryant Mole (Wayland)
Splitting Up K Bryant Mole (Wayland)
Step Families K Bryant Mole (Wayland)
Divorce A Grunsell (Franklin Watts)

Fostering/in care

Key Stage 1
Bruce's Story M Thom et al (Children's Society)
Going into Care B Orritt (Children's Society)
My New Family Althea (Dinosaur)

Key Stage 2
How it Feels to be Adopted J Krementz (Gollancz)
The Pinballs B Byers (Puffin)

Adoption

Key Stage 1
The New Sister A de Menezes (Blackbird)

Key Stage 2
Michael and the Jumble Sale Cat M Newman (Hamish Hamilton)
Adoption K Bryant Mole (Wayland)

Death and dying

Key Stage 1
Badger's Parting Gifts S Varley (Picture Lion)
Grandma's Bill M Waddell (Walker)
Remembering Mum G Perkins & L Morris (A & C Black)
Come Back Grandma S Limb (Bodley Head)
Emma's Cat Dies N Snell (Hamish Hamilton)
Flowers for Samantha L Parr (Methuen)
Granpa J Burningham (Cape)
Gran's Grave W Green (Lion)
Nana Upstairs and Nana Downstairs T de Paola (Methuen)
When Uncle Bob Died L Kopper (Althea)
The Very Best of Friends M Wild (Bodley Head)

Key Stage 2
The Man Who Wanted to Live for Ever S Hastings (Walker)
A Taste of Blackberries D Buchanan Smith (Heinnemann)
The Fall of Freddie the Leaf L Buseaglia Holt (Rinehart & Winston)

A Summer to Die L Lowry (Collins Lion)
Cousins V Hamilton (Gollancz)
Daddy's Chair S Lanton (Kar-Ben Copies)
Death K Bryant Mole (Wayland)
Goodbye Max H Keller (Walker Books)
Goodbye Rune M Kaldhol (Kane/Miller)
Grandpa's Slide Show D Gould (Viking/Kestrel)
I Had a Friend Named Peter J Cohn (William Morrow)
I'll Always Love You H Wilhelm (Hodder/Stoughton)
Kirsty's Kite C Stilz (Lion)
The Tenth Good Thing About Barney J Viorst (Collins)
Death K Bryant Mole (Wayland)
Remembering Grandad G Padvan (Child's Play)

Bullying

Key Stage 1
The Story of Ferdinand M Leaf (Hippo Books)
Bailey the Big Bully L Boyd (Puffin)

Key Stage 2
Bullying K Bryant Mole (Wayland)
All My Men B Ashley (Puffin)

Abuse

Key Stage 1
No More Secrets for Me O Wachter (Kestrel)
What's Wrong With Bottoms? J Hessell (Hutchinson)

Key Stage 2
Child Abuse K Bryant Mole (Wayland)

Emotions

Anger

Key Stage 1
How the Witch Got Alf C Annett (Franklin Watts)
Millions of Cats W Gag (Faber/Penguin)
Different Dragons J Little (Puffin)
Tall Inside J Richardson (Puffin)
Where the Wild Things Are M Sendak (Puffin/Bodley Head)

Key Stage 2
Theo Runs Away O Hartling (Anderson Press)
Joey R Van der Meer (Heinemann)
Angry Arthur H Oram et al (Anderson)
Where the Wild Things Are M Sendak (Picture Puffin)

Fear

Key Stage 1
The Owl Who Was Afraid of the Dark J Tomlinson (Puffin/Methuen)
Andrew's First Flight D McPhaill (Puffin)
Who's Afraid of the Dark? C Bonsall (World's Work)
I Won't Go There Again S Hill (Walker)

Key Stage 2
The Hospital Scares Me P Hogan (Blackwell)
There's a Nightmare in my Cupboard M Mayer (Dent)

Jealousy

Key Stage 1
John Brown, Rose and the Midnight Cat J Wagner (Kestrel/Picture Puffin)
That's My Baby V Konigslow (Annick Press)

Key Stage 2
I Hate My Sister W Jackman (Firefly)

Special times

Key Stage 1
Amoko and the Party S Appiah (Andre Deutsch)
Sammy and the Telly O Elliott (Andre Deutsch)
Colin's Baptism O Bennett (Hamish Hamilton)
From Me to You P Rogers (Orchard Books)
Something Special E Rodda (Young Puffin)
Granny's Quilt P Ives (Hamish Hamilton)

Key Stage 2
At the Crossroads R Isadora (Red Fox)
The Patchwork Quilt V Flournoy (Picture Puffin)
Bobbi's New Year J Solomon (Hamish Hamilton)
Kate's Party J Solomon (Hamish Hamilton)
Berron's Tooth J Solomon (Hamish Hamilton)
Shabnam's Day Out J Solomon (Hamish Hamilton)
The Joy of Birth C Jessel (Methuen)
Being Born S Kitzinger (Dorling)

Special Educational Needs

Asthma

Key Stage 1
Jane has Asthma N Snell (Hamish Hamilton)

Key Stage 2
Mummy, Why Can't I Breathe? P Watson (Angus and Robertson)

Down's syndrome

Key Stage 1
Ben V Shennan (Bodley Head)

Key Stage 2
I have Down's Syndrome B Pettenuzzo (Franklin Watts)
I am Louise A Rooke (Learning Development Aids)
Jane Shops at the Supermarket I Smallwood (Collins)
Our Brother has Down's Syndrome S Cairo (Annick Press)

Epilepsy

Key Stage 2
What Difference Does it Make Danny? F Young (OUP)
The Detective's Story P Rogan (Quay)
I Have Epilepsy B Pettenuzzo (Franklin Watts)

Hearing difficulties

Key Stage 1
I Can't Hear Like You Althea (Dinosaur)
The Boy Who Couldn't Hear F Bloom (Bodley Head)

Claire and Emma D (Peter Black)
Peter Gets a Hearing Aid N Snell (Hamish Hamilton)
I Have a Sister, My Sister is Deaf J Peterson (Harper and Row)

Key Stage 2
Journey from Peppermint Street M De Jong (Collins)
David in Silence V Robinson (Deutsch)
Lisa and Her Soundless World E Levine (Human Science)
Finding a Common Language T Bergman (Gareth Stevens Children's Books)

Severe learning difficulties
Key Stage 1
Don't Forget Tom H Larsen (Black)
One Little Girl J Fassler (Human Science)

Key Stage 2
Boss of the Pool B Klein (Kestrel)
We Laugh, We Love, We Cry T Bergman (Gareth Stevens Children's Books)

Physical disability
Key Stage 1
Rachel E Fanshawe (Bodley Head)
Janet at School P White (A&C Black)

Key Stage 2
Alexander in Trouble & Other Stories S Burke (Bodley Head)
Come on David, Jump D Huttner (Angus and Robertson)
Mark's Wheelchair Adventures C Jessell (Methuen)
I Have Cerebral Palsy B Pettenuzzo (Franklin Watts)
I Have Spina Bifida B Pettenuzzo (Franklin Watts)
I Have Cystic Fibrosis B Pettenuzzo (Franklin Watts)
I Have Muscular Dystrophy B Pettenuzzo (Franklin Watts)
On Our Own Terms T Bergman (Gareth Stevens Children's Books)

Speech difficulties
Key Stage 1
Fiona Finds her Tongue D Hendry (Puffin)
John the Mouse who Learned to Read B Randell (Puffin)
I Can't Talk Like You Althea (Dinosaur)
Shy Charles R Wells (Lion)

Key Stage 2
Hoo Ming's Discovery M Cockett (Hamish Hamilton)

Visual difficulties
Key Stage 1
Sally Can't See P Patterson (A&C Black)
Watch Out, Ronald Gordon P Reilly Gief (Kestrel)
My Sister Katie C Wright (Scripture Union)

Key Stage 2
Fingers That See T Bergman (Kestrel)
Cowboy Surprise W Wise (Hamish Hamilton)
Maria C Brighton (Faber)
I am Blind B Pettenuzzo (Franklin Watts)
Seeing in Special Ways T Bergman (Gareth Stevens Children's Books

Death and Dying

Death and Dying

Coping with the death of a pet or somebody close to us can be one of the most distressing events with which we are faced. Whilst it is recognised that there will be specific times when a school community wishes to reflect upon the life and death of someone they have known, if the subject is incorporated into RE study units children are helped to explore some of the emotions associated with loss and change in their lives.

The activity is best suited to a group who are well-known to the teacher.

Objectives
- To help children to explore their own experiences of loss and change
- To help children to explore their own feelings about death and dying and to express their emotions
- To help children become aware of other people's emotions
- To give children the opportunity to develop some strategies for coping when sad things happen

Resources
- A large circular tablecloth
- A collection of objects from the natural world which have once been alive, e.g. sea shells, dried flowers and leaves, seed pods, dried roots, bark, small animal skeletons
- A bunch of seedless grapes
- A dish of raisins
- Story about death/dying (from the list of stories section on Death and Dying)

Setting the scene
Display the objects from the natural world so that they provide a focal point which will arouse the interest of the children.

The activity
Ask several children to select an item and to feel it very carefully. What is it like to touch? Where was it found? Has it always been exactly as it is now? It is hoped that pupils will decide that the objects are dead or that they are part of something which has died. Encourage words to describe the objects such as still, cold, dry.

Read or tell one of the stories suggested in the list of stories (section Death and Dying), providing pictures, visual aids etc, where appropriate. How did the children feel when they listened to the story? Invite each child to think of a word, phrase, or symbols which describe the feeling. Talk about the feelings.

Offer each child a grape and ask them first to look at it and then to feel the texture of it in their mouth. What does it taste like? Encourage words such as smooth, sweet, juicy. Offer each child a raisin, and again ask them to take a good look at it before putting it into their mouth. What does the raisin feel like? Is it the same texture as the grape? Are there words or symbols which describe the raisin? Does anyone know what the raisin was once like?

Explain that although the raisin is 'dead', and it is shrivelled and brown, it still tastes very good. Although we are sad when someone close to us dies and their body becomes useless, the memory of the good times which we spent with them can never be taken away.

Sensory learning experiences
Using the display described in the activities for Death and Dying which is also illustrated in the drawing, pupils might be encouraged to participate in learning experiences.

Hold a piece of dry bark in your hand and feel its texture and pattern. Trace the grooves with your fingers.
Hold a sea shell to your ear. Can you hear anything?
Explore the hole in the seashell with your fingers.
Scrunch dry leaves with your hands and hear the crackling noise.
Feel the tickle of dry roots across the top of your hand.
Gently hold the star fish and feel how fragile it is.
Look at the beautiful shapes of the seed heads and seed pods.
Notice nothing moves on the display.

New Beginnings

New beginnings are usually thought of as exciting, positive times, with new circumstances to look forward to, but for all of us it can also be a time of anxiety, and children need to develop positive attitudes towards change.

From their first day in school, children experience new feelings as they begin to settle down in an unfamiliar environment, but in a warm supportive atmosphere they will soon develop a sense of security and trust. However, it is important to acknowledge that any initial feelings of insecurity are very 'real' and that it is permissible to show emotions, and to learn to acknowledge them, for it is only when pupils 'own' their emotions that they come to terms with them.

The activity is best suited to pupils who have been in school at least a year.

Objectives

- To encourage children to reflect on meaningful 'milestones' in their own lives
- To help children to develop positive attitudes towards new situations and new ideas
- To encourage children to develop strategies for coping with new circumstances at home and at school.
- To help children to develop an awareness of self in relation to other people

Resources

- A large circular tablecloth
- A selection of new-born baby clothes
- A large picture of a baby and pictures of children's younger siblings (NB make sure you are familiar with the names of the children in the pictures)
- A time-line on which symbols have been drawn to mark significant events in children's lives from birth until the present day (special events might include: birthdays; initiation ceremonies; new teeth; staying away from home for a night; starting school)
- Life-size outlines of some of the group of children, drawn on paper
- A story which has a human experience theme, for example, *Peter's Chair* (see list of stories section Myself and Relationships)

Before the activity

Make 'time-lines' with children on large sheets of paper, drawing symbols which represent events which the children consider important in their lives from birth to the present day. Make life-size outlines of children on large sheets of paper.

Setting the scene

Display the baby clothes together with some items used to care for a baby, for example, a baby bath, nappy, potty, feeding bottle. Place the poster in a prominent place.

The activity

Explain that the theme of the activity is New Beginnings. Read *Peter's Chair* and invite children to comment on what it is like to have a new baby brother or sister.

Talk to children about their picture outlines, mentioning personal characteristics such as hair colour, body size. Ask whether the children with the pictures have always looked exactly as they are now. What has changed? Talk about growth and show how tiny the displayed baby clothes are. Remind all the children that they were once babies.

Share the photographs of younger brothers and sisters, being sure to mention their names.

Invite the children with time-lines to share how they felt at significant times in their lives.

Talk about how children felt on their first day at school. Did anyone 'special' help them and offer friendship?

Encourage pupils to be kind and helpful to the children and adults who are new to school now.

Journeys

The theme is one which is relevant to all of us, regardless of culture, ability or creed. We all have a life journey to make but not all of us are prepared to travel in the company of other people who will help us realise our ambitions and reach our milestones.

Faith has a lot to do with a topic on journeys. Indeed many religions speak of themselves as a 'path' or a 'way' where followers engage in a 'spiritual' search. The analogy of a journey has rich potential: there may be marking of stages on a journey; there are paths which set out the ways; there are places of pilgrimage.

Objectives

- To help children explore their own life journey from birth to the present time
- To encourage children to reflect on the importance of preparing for a journey to a special place.
- To encourage children to develop positive attitudes towards signs, symbols, artefacts and mementoes which have special significance to pilgrims

Resources

- A display of holiday postcards, travel brochures and a guidebook or souvenir book from a place of pilgrimage, e.g. a cathedral or shrine
- Children's writing or art work about life journeys, e.g. birth, being a baby, becoming part of a school family, starting a job, ageing, dying
- A selection of items which are 'special' to children and which they might choose to take on a journey, e.g. a teddy bear or soft toy, a favourite book
- A suitcase or large travel bag with a few items inside which suggest the owner is going away on a journey
- A selection of religious artefacts which might be either taken on a pilgrimage or brought home as a reminder of the visit (*NB* These should be carefully wrapped and introduced during the activity)
- A large, brightly coloured circular tablecloth

Setting the scene

Before the pupils arrive, set up the display with the suitcase or travel bag in the centre revealing some of the contents.

The activity

Once the children are seated around the display, ask if they are able to guess the theme of the activity.

Talk about the contents of the luggage and ask for suggestions about the kind of journey which the person might be going on. What would the children choose to take?

Introduce the children's writing or art work, and talk about life journeys. Explain that many people visit places where important events have taken place or where notable people have lived. Draw children's attention to the guidebook or souvenir book and carefully unpack some of the 'precious' reminders which pilgrims have kept as a reminder of their faith journey.

End the activity by asking pupils to help carefully 'pack' away the 'special' objects.

LIFE JOURNEYS

FIRST STOP - BIRTH
I am a child who is not yet born
And I lie in my mother's womb.
All I do is lie and wait
And hope to be born soon.

I sit here quiet and still
I am quite alone.
I cannot speak yet
So I cannot even moan.

Now I am moving
The birth is taking place.
The nurse dresses me in towelling
My mother dresses me in lace.

SECOND STOP - BEING A BABY
I would want to be a baby so I can wake Mummy up in the night. Maa! Maa! Mummy will give me a bottle. In the morning Mummy will give me my breakfast. I wouldn't want to be a baby because I would get told off.

THIRD STOP - STARTING SCHOOL
I remember the day I started school. It was big and strange. I couldn't do the writing because I couldn't hold the pencil!

FOURTH STOP - STARTING A JOB
It is very hard to get a job. Some jobs are easy and some jobs are not. There are caring jobs like being a doctor or a nurse.
There are keeping people safe jobs like police people and firemen.
There are business jobs like a secretary and a manager.
There are children jobs like being a mother or a teacher or a nanny.

FIFTH STOP - GETTING OLDER
I like old people. My gran has wrinkled skin, warm hands and crinkles around her eyes. When I am old I shall tell a story like my grampy does and then I shall think about my children.

SIXTH STOP - THE END
Dying is a very sad thing. Sometimes you die because you are ill. Sometimes children die too. Dead means you are dead for ever. But some people believe that when you die you can start up a new life in heaven. So it is the beginning of a life in another place.

Our taxis take us home

OUR JOURNEYS

Pilgrimages are often undertaken by people in order to give expression to their faith or to be associated in faith with significant events. But pilgrimages are also symbols of events in the journey of life. Year 3 pupils in a London Borough special school have drawn and written about journeys which are important to them. The spelling remains unchanged.

Sometimes people go on a trip to a special place.

The Good shepherd had to travel to find the lost shep.

Me and my arntea we went to israel.

I pertend my cat and me can go away to a majic plays.

When you die you goes in a blach van. It is a ride in a box.

We went to the place could the zoe.

CHAPTER 10

Religious Artefacts

For thousands of years, humankind has used religious objects and symbols. Artefacts may be central to worship, or used to help direct attention. Sometimes they provide comfort or inspiration, for example, a holy picture, scarred by years of being folded in a pocket, or a Seder plate which has been present in a Jewish family at the re-enactment of the Exodus story for generations. Their value is in the symbolic meaning they have for their owners and in the doors which they open to believers and to those who learn from them.

In school, artefacts help children to explore questions and beliefs, giving them the opportunity to learn from direct experience. They may also help to foster communication skills, and they lend themselves as inspiration for the creative and expressive arts in poems, stories and songs. It is important that all children see and touch religious artefacts, sensing their visual and tactile qualities, for their presence brings a dimension to religion which it is difficult to create through even the best posters, videos and books. But their value does not end here, because they are objects of reflection, used as a focal point in rituals and celebrations, or as aids to prayer and meditation.

But how far should religious objects be used in the context of Religious Education? Perhaps the golden rule is that their use should be to encourage reflection rather than devotion. As teachers, we must tread with great care. The attitudes which we convey to pupils, by the way in which we talk about and use artefacts, speak a thousand words to children.

The lists of religious artefacts have been divided into those most commonly used by religious communities in Great Britain. Purchasing can be an exciting and rewarding experience. Many local faith communities will have shops where they can be bought. The following suppliers are also recommended.

Artefact Suppliers

Artefacts to Order (Tel.: 01945 587452)

Collections of religious artefacts, arranged in sets.

Articles of Faith Bury Business Centre, Kay Street, Bury BL9 6BU (Tel.: 0161 705 1878)
Colour brochure of artefacts relating to each principal religion. Also some collections of artefacts based on a theme, e.g. Festivals of Light; Passover.

History in Evidence Unit 4, Park Road, Holmewood, Chesterfield S42 5UY (Tel.: 0800 318686)
Colour brochure with pictures of artefacts relating to principal religions. Artefacts may be ordered separately or in collections.

SPCK Bookshop 7 St Peter's Street, Canterbury CT1 3AT (Tel.: 01227 462881)

Suppliers of Christian artefacts. NB Check local telephone directory for nearest SPCK shop.

Tantra Designs Gas Ferry Road, Bristol BS1 6UN
Buddhist images, incense, posters, cards etc.

Little India 91 The Broadway, Southall, Middx UB1 1LN (Tel.: 0181 5712029)
Highly recommended for mail order or direct purchase of Hindu, Sikh and Muslim artefacts.

Muslim Information Services 223 Seven Sisters Road, London N4 2DA (Tel.: 0171 2725170)
Mail order and direct purchase of Muslim artefacts.

Jewish Memorial Council Bookshop Woburn House, Upper Woburn Place, Tavistock Square, London WC1H 0EP (Tel.: 0171 387 3952 x 140)
Mail order of Jewish artefacts offering 10% discount for school orders.

Christian artefacts might include:

Chalice (for wine at the Eucharist)
Paten (for bread or wafers at the Eucharist)
Wafers (unconsecrated)
Individual wine glass used in Communion services in Free Churches
Basket used for the bread in Free Church Communion services
White tablecloth used to cover the Communion table
Icon
Bibles: family; Gideon New Testament; children's
Order of Service books: Anglican; Book of Common Prayer; Wedding Service; Funeral Service; Baptism Service; Ordination Service; Confirmation Service
Prayer Books: Anglican; Roman Catholic Missal; Orthodox; Free Churches
Prayer cards
Hassock (Kneeler)
Hymn books; carol sheets;
Crosses: wooden; pendent; crucifix; celtic; palm
Baptism gown
Icthus badge (fish)
Dove badge
Statue of the Madonna and Child
Badges of Christian organisations
Clerical collar worn by ordained priests and ministers
Rosary
Cards: Easter; Christmas; First Communion; Confirmation; Ordination; Wedding; Sympathy
Confirmation Veil
Incense (Prinknash)
Candles: baptism; votive; memorial; vigil; first communion; Advent
Advent calendar
Thurible (incense burner)

Hindu artefacts might include:

Aum (Om) symbol representing God
Spices (saffron, cumin and crushed chillies) and container
Henna
Joss sticks (incense sticks)
Packet of cotton wicks (for arti or diva lamps)
Arti lamp; divas
Janeu (sacred thread worn by Hindus who study under a guru)
Rakhi (bracelet made out of silk or cotton)
Puja set and tray
Tarbhana (large copper dish used for worship)
Beaker for holy water

Aachman (spoon)
Copper dish (saucer-shaped) for money offerings
Mala (circle of stringed prayer beads)
Kirtan or Bhajans (copies of devotional hymns)
Har (garland used for decoration, adornment, ceremonies and festivals)
Kumkum (red powder)
Bindi (red spots for forehead)
Dhoti (garment made of natural fibre worn by males)
Pictures of Hindu gods
Figures of Hindu deities (Ganesha; Hanuman; Krishna; Lakshmi; Parvati; Shiva; Vishnu; Rama; Sita)
Book of Rangoli patterns

Sikh artefacts might include:

Kirpan (small sword)
Sling for kirpan
Kangha (small comb)
Kachera (white shorts)
Kara (bracelet)
Ik Onkar (Sikh badge)
Khanda badge
Pictures of Gurus
Garlands
Book of readings from the Guru Granth Sahib
Romalla (cover for Guru Granth Sahib)
Fabric for turban or a turban (pagri)
Cards for Festivals, e.g. Guru Nanak's birthday; Baisakhi

Islamic artefacts might include:

Prayer mat
Prayer hat (topi)
Subhah (prayer beads)
Qur'an (translation)
Qur'an stand and cover
Qur'an case
Posters of Qur'anic verses
Compass to find direction of Makkah
Id cards (e.g. Id-ul-Fitr)
Bindi (worn to show a woman is married)
Hijab (veil worn by some women)
Example of Muslim calligraphy

Jewish artefacts might include:

Kiddush cup (wine goblet for Shabbat)
Shabbat candlesticks and candles (and a travelling pair if possible)
Order of service for Shabbat
Challah loaf (plaited loaf used at Shabbat)
Challah bread cover

Spice box for Shabbat
Tallit (prayer shawl)
Siddur (daily prayer book)
Tzizit (fringed undervest worn by some Jewish males)
Tefillin (small leather boxes containing passages from the Torah)
Kippah (yamulkah or capel) – male head covering
Mezuzah and scroll
Tenach (Jewish Bible)
Sefer Torah scroll (five books of Moses written on parchment)
Yad (for pointing when reading from scrolls)
Menorah
Dreidel
Magen David (Star of David)
Seder dish (Passover dish)
Hagadah (Pesach service book)
Pesach cards (Passover cards)
Passover napkins
Matzot (in the red box marked 'for Passover use')
Matzah cover
Jewish New Year card
Bar Mitzvah card (male initiation)
Bat Mitzvah card (female initiation)
Ketubah (marriage certificate)
Menorah (branched candlestick)
Candles for menorah
Gregger (noise-maker used in Purim celebrations)
Shofar (ram's horn for Rosh Hashanah)
Memorial light

Buddhist artefacts might include:

Dorje (Tibetan diamond thunderbolt)
Ghanta (bell)
Incense and holder
Joss sticks
Mandala
Mala (prayer beads)
Pictures or images of the Buddha
Prayer Wheel
Wheel

Chinese artefacts might include:

Fans
Chinese newspaper
Lantern decorations
Wall plaques
Chopsticks
Taper candles
Porcelain dishes
Porcelain spoons
Astrological chart
Dragon puppets
Incense
Bean sprouts
Tea
Noodles
Wall-hangings
Children's embroidered jackets, hats, etc.

References

Bell, G. (1994) *Action Research, Special Needs and School Development.* London: David Fulton.

Brown, E. (1991) *Opening Children's Eyes to Worship.* London: The National Society (Church of England) for Promoting Religious Education.

Brown, E. (1993) *Mixed Blessings – The Special Child in Your School.* London: The National Society (Church of England) for Promoting Religious Education.

Brown, E. (1995) 'Circles of Growth' in *PMLD Link,* Issue 22.

Brown E. (1995) 'Learning about religious belief in special schools', in *World Religions in Education.* Surrey: New Look Translations.

Carpenter, B. (1995) 'Building an Inclusive Curriculum', in Ashcroft, K. and Palacio, D. (Eds) (1995) *The Primary Teachers Guide to the National Curriculum.* London: Falmer.

Chailey Heritage School *Charter of Children's Rights.* East Sussex: Chailey Heritage School.

DFE (1994) *Code of Practice on the Identification and Assessment of Special Educational Needs.* Department for Education and the Welsh Office.

DFE (1994) Circular 1/94 *Religious Education and Collective Worship.* Department for Education.

Dowell, J. and Nutt, M. (1995) 'An Approach to Religious Education at Piper Hill School', in *PMLD Link,* Issue 22.

Education (Schools) Act (1993) HMSO.

Education Reform Act (1988) HMSO.

Goss, P. (1995) 'Opening Up: The Inner Lives of Individuals with PMLD', in *PMLD Link,* Issue 22.

Longhorn, F. (1993) *Religious Education for Very Special Children.* Isle of Man: ORCA Publications.

NCC (1993) *Spiritual and Moral Development – a Discussion Document.* London: National Curriculum Council.

OFSTED (1993) *Framework for Inspection of Schools.* London: OFSTED.

RESPECT – Journal of the Special Religious Education Network, edited by Brown, A. and Brown, E. Available from: 7 Elyham, Purley-on-Thames, Berkshire RG8 8EN.

SCAA (1994) *Model Syllabuses for Religious Education.* London: Schools Curriculum and Assessment Authority.

SCAA (1995) *Planning the Curriculum at Key Stages 1 and 2.* London: Schools Curriculum and Assessment Authority.

Vulliamy, G. and Webb, R. (Eds) (1992) *Teacher Research and Special Educational Needs.* London: David Fulton Publishers.

Bibliography

The following books provide information about the principal religions. Schools should choose from each section and keep a record of selected titles in the documentation which provides information about resources for Religious Education.

Christianity

A First Bible: Old Testament (1988) Simon & Schuster, ISBN: 0 671 69895 8

New Testament (1989) Simon & Schuster, ISBN: 0 671 69680 7

Tomie de Paola's Book of Bible Stories (1990) Hodder & Stoughton, ISBN: 0 340 50131 6

Christians – Through the Ages – Around the World (1994) Lion Publishing, ISBN: 0 7459 2516 2

Be a Church Detective (1992) Church House Publishing, ISBN: 0 7151 4790 0

Christianity: Religions Through Festivals (1989) Longman, ISBN: 0 582 31791 6

I am an Anglican (1986) Franklin Watts, ISBN: 0 86313 427 0

I am a Pentecostal (1986) Franklin Watts, ISBN: 0 86313 428 9

I am a Roman Catholic (1985) Franklin Watts, ISBN: 0 86313 258 8

I am a Greek Orthodox (1985) Franklin Watts, ISBN: 0 86313 259 6

Judaism

I am a Jew (1984) Franklin Watts, ISBN: 0 86313 139 5

Our Culture (1988) Franklin Watts, ISBN: 0 86313 671 0

The Westhill Project R.E. 5-16 – JEWS 1 & 2 (1990) Stanley Thornes, ISBN: 1 871402 18 2

Ten Good Rules (1991) Kar-Ben Copies Inc, ISBN: 0 929371 28 3

Mazal-Tov: A Jewish Wedding (1988) Hamish Hamilton, ISBN: 0 241 12269 4

Celebrations: Sam's Passover (1985) A & C Black, ISBN: 0 7136 2646 1

A Happy New Year (1987) Hamish Hamilton, ISBN: 0 241 12047 0

Hanukkah – The Festival of Lights (1989) Walker Books, ISBN: 0 7445 1260 3
Passover Seder for Primary Schools Wandsworth Borough Council

Islam

Leaders of Religion – Muhammad (1985) Oliver & Boyd, ISBN: 0 05 003913 X
The Prophets (1992) IQRA Trust, ISBN: 1 85679 901 8
Growing Up in Islam (1990) Longman, ISBN: 0 582 00287 7
I am a Muslim (1985) Franklin Watts, ISBN: 0 86313 1387
Festival! Ramadan and Eid-ul-Fitr (1986) Macmillan Education, ISBN: 0 333 37902 0
The Life of Muhammad (1987) Wayland, ISBN: 0 85078 904 4
Stories from the Muslim World (1987) Macdonald, ISBN: 0 356 11563 1
Muslim Festivals (1990) RMEP

Hinduism

I am a Hindu (1984) Franklin Watts, ISBN: 0 86313 168 9
The Hindu World (1989) Macdonald, ISBN: 0 356 07521
Holi: Hindu Festival of Spring (1987) Hamish Hamilton, ISBN: 0 241 11986 3
Growing up in Hinduism (1990) Longman, ISBN: 0582 002850
Indian Food and Drink (1986) Wayland, ISBN: 0 85078 897 8
Dance of Shiva (1989) Hamish Hamilton, ISBN: 0 241 12550 2
Journey with the Gods (1987) Mantra, ISBN: 0 94679 80 4
The Story of the Hindus (1989) OUP, ISBN: 0 521 26261 8
Religions through Festivals – Hinduism (1988) Longman, ISBN: 0 582 31788 6
Festivals – Hindu Festivals (1985) Wayland, ISBN: 0 85078 5715
Festival! Diwali (1986) Macmillan Education, ISBN: 0 333 37899 7
Religious Stories – Hindu Stories (1986) Wayland, ISBN: 0 85078 863 3
Stories from – The Hindu World (1986) Macdonald, ISBN: 0 356 11509 7

Sikhism

Teaching R.E. – Sikhism 5-11 (1994) CEM, ISBN: 1 85100 073 X
Guru Nanak and the Sikh Gurus (1987) Wayland, ISBN: 0 85078 906 0
Pavan is a Sikh A & C Black, ISBN: 0 7136 1721 7
Stories from – The Sikh World (1987) Macdonald, ISBN: 0 356 13165 3
Growing up in Sikhism (1990) Longman, ISBN: 0 582 002869
I am a Sikh Franklin Watts, ISBN: 0 86313 147 6

Buddhism

Buddhist Stories (1986) Wayland, ISBN: 0 85078 864 1
The Buddha and the Elephant (1989) Mary Glasgow Publications, ISBN: 1 85234 2749
Our Culture – Buddhist (1988) Franklin Watts, ISBN: 0 86313 6745
The Life of the Buddha (1987) Wayland, ISBN: 0 85078 903 6
I am a Buddhist Franklin Watts, ISBN: 0 86313 261 8
Festivals of the Buddha (1984) RMEP, ISBN: 0 08 030611 X
Prince Siddhartha (1980) Wisdom, ISBN: 0 86171 016 9
Buddhism (1986) Wayland, ISBN: 0 85078 722 X
Buddhist Festivals (1985) Wayland, ISBN: 085078 572 3

Teachers will also find *RESPECT,* a termly journal for Religious Education to pupils of all abilities at Key Stages 1-3, a valuable resource. Details from: Erica Brown, 7 Elyham, Purley-on-Thames, Berkshire RG8 8EN. Phone and fax: 01734 843664.